TWENTY GIRLS TO ENVY ME

Selected Poems of Orit Gidali

Modern Middle East Literatures in Translation Series

TWENTY GIRLS TO ENVY ME

Selected Poems of
Orit Gidali

Translated, edited, and introduced
by Marcela Sulak

CENTER FOR MIDDLE EASTERN STUDIES
THE UNIVERSITY OF TEXAS AT AUSTIN

CONTENTS

INTRODUCTION

And I now say yes to the epidural, and yes to the aspirin, and yes to the fallow years of shmita, to the talent wasted on washing bottles and making the bed, yes to the belly that hardens like a tree, and yes to the slingshot, the constant balls of worry the hand releases, yes and yes

—FROM "ETROG"

Orit Gidali was born in Israel in 1974, months after the simultaneous surprise attacks on the country from the north and the south that initiated the Yom Kippur War and revived acute existential fears linked to the Holocaust thirty years before. She was born into a society skeptical of its leadership and into a culture that was beginning to shift its focus from the collective to the individual. The collective front, symbolized by the socialist kibbutz founders of the State of Israel, was beginning a slow crumble, and on opposite edges, the nongovernmental forces of Peace Now and the extraparliamentary forces of the settlers of the Gush Emunim were forming. Today, as the opportunities for true dialogue diminish, and states become increasingly polarized, and more energy is expended in excluding than including, in saying no, rather than yes, Orit Gidali's poetry bursts onto the literary landscape on a pulse of *yes*.

Gidali stands somewhat apart from the generation of poets born after 1973, whose focus is generally on the individual as an individual, rather than as a member of a community. The previous generation of Israeli poets, such as Yehuda Amichai, a major influence on Gidali, often use national epic discourse to describe personal lyrical experiences. These poets do so in order to carve out the possibility for human agency in an overdetermined political, religious, and existential environment.

Amichai always recognizes that the individual is bound to "all the generations before" that have "donated me bit by bit," as he puts it.[1] Like Amichai, Gidali recognizes that the individual arises as a temporary wave in a sea of generations. The individual's active being will impact those who come after, as well as those who came before, performing a Jewish version of T. S. Eliot's "Tradition and the Individual Talent." The characters of Gidali's poetry understand that they exist in a particular preestablished geopolitical landscape, and that this landscape marks them.

When Gidali and I spoke about the impact that growing up in Israel in the aftermath of the Yom Kippur War had on her poetry, she explained:

> I was born after a war; my father fought in many wars, and I am a mother of sons. As such, I am part of the Israeli *danse macabre*, a society that is tied to a violent conflict, which influences my existential anxiety and my understanding that there is a gap between the inside of the home, with its purity and beauty, and the violence outside. I feel helpless, ashamed, and sad in the face of the political situation, and these feelings take deep root in my poetry.[2]

In Gidali's work, the domestic sphere is the stage on which the drama of the geopolitical is revealed on an individual scale. For example, in the poem beginning "Toward morning I found a blind cat," the insomniac speaker's treatment of a kitten takes on unbearable significance, as if the kitten's fate were bound up with the fate of her future soldier son. At the same time, the poem's present conflict is an echo of the conflicts that took place in the world of the speaker's parents and grandparents during the Holocaust and the pogroms of Europe:

(camp refugees equal refugee camps, heaps of what we will become if we don't stand strong), what caused the silent sobbings and the fear of the dark (*soldiers   soldiers   fire our village devoured*)

Since the speaker's son is now a member of the more powerful side of the most recent manifestation of an ancient conflict, the speaker superimposes the phrases that originated in Yiddish-language poems and reportage about nineteenth-century pogroms and the twentieth-century Holocaust upon twenty-first-century Palestinian refugee camps in Israeli occupied territories. Thus, she acknowledges that the cycle of violence and war continues, and she registers her reluctance to contribute to it.

Often lyric poetry has been equated with a retreat into the private sphere, where it is monological, and the speaker is answerable only to the self. Gidali's withdrawal from a predetermined social narrative is one answer to the dilemma of the *danse macabre* Gidali describes above, but Gidali's domestic space is by no means a private retreat. For her, the domestic is always already inhabited by "the other." Her most private and most domestic poems are multivoiced because in the house of Gidali's poetry, the body and the language and the mouths that speak it are haunted—or perhaps simultaneously inhabited—by the speaker's ancestors, by the Jewish patriarchs and matriarchs. And the language of Gidali's poetry shows the traces of where it came from, just as the land she inhabits still retains the traces of the Temple and the City of David. The home is further haunted by the ghost of a woman to whom the speaker's husband was previously married, and by the "others" that have attempted to destroy the speaker's ancestors, relatives, and neighbors, from the Egyptian exodus to the Yom Kippur War. Also present are the soldiers—other mothers' children that the speaker's soldier children might one day kill in war. There is no "retreat" into the domestic.

But if the characters of Gidali's poems are responsible for actions committed before they were born, and for situations that they inherited, so, too, do they partake in a kind of holiness that is given, not earned, described in the poem "We Could Have Lived So Well, You Say, and Gaze at Her, Still Pretty," which depicts the tranquility of the Sabbath falling upon the secular world of the Sharon Plain:

> In a little while Shabbat in the Sharon, and traffic lights take
> off their red, and the laces unravel and yield the bare foot,
> and the records of the word gather into a book and rest from
> their anxiousness to break, and the change in the wallet
> emphasizes the victory of the many and the small.

As Yitzhak Laor says in his 2009 *Ha'aretz* review, in the world of Gidali's poetry, "everything belongs to everyone, and nothing belongs to anyone."[3]

Israeli critical response to Gidali's poetry often includes a weighty biographical element, sometimes noting that one might, of course, read Gidali without knowing her biography, but that doing so would deprive the reader of a crucial element.[4] The "crucial element" they mean is the knowledge the opening poem, "Songs to a Dead Woman," in Gidali's second book, *Closing In*, which addresses a suicide whose daughter is being raised by the speaker, is based on events from the poet's personal life. I myself disagree; there is almost no contemporary or modern Israeli poet who does not draw quite obviously from autobiography for artistic material. Consider poets Shimon Adaf, Yehuda Amichai, Leah Goldberg, Yona Wallach, Erez Biton, and even writers of fiction such as Amos Oz, Meir Shalev, Etgar Keret, and David Grossman. In this, Israel is much like the West. The turn to the individual in Israeli writing came, quite naturally, after existential fears over the establishment of the State of Israel had diminished. At this point, it is generally recognized that individual experiences are part of the context of the founding and existence of the State of Israel.

Lyrical poetry, despite the biographical fallacy it might sometimes encourage, is most certainly an incisive tool for reading a society's deeply held beliefs and unacknowledged attitudes, for reading the social silence beneath the individual articulation. Gidali's poetry reveals a society haunted by the Holocaust, individual ambivalence about one's children's military service, national attitudes toward motherhood, and the primordial rivalry between Rachel and Leah.

The reason we say literature feels authentic is that it accurately captures what we imagine *could have happened*; it depicts a situation in a manner of which we can conceive. The best poetry allows us to image what before was inconceivable to us; it gives expression to what had hitherto been unutterable—usually because it had been censored by the greater culture from which it grew. We censor what we consider irrelevant or threatening.

Often literature written by women (especially when it is also about women) is sidelined because it is deemed irrelevant to the national mythos of many nations. On the Israeli scene, the masculinity of the image of the fighting sabra, or native-born Israeli, who will never be victimized again, is amplified by the fact that, until the end of the nineteenth century—that is, until Hebrew began to be spoken by a majority living in Palestine—Hebrew was a language for men. It was the language of prayer. Diaspora women, who were not required to pray in a minyan and who were not educated in yeshivas in Hebrew, read, spoke, and wrote Yiddish (or Ladino, Arabic, Russian, Polish, French, or German).

Likewise, literature in general, and women's literature in particular, is censored when it is deemed threatening to cultural norms and societal mores. Women usually censor themselves more effectively than publishers. An American example of this censorship is described in the Jewish American poet Rachel Zucker's collection, *Museum of Accidents*. Zucker's speaker notes and rebukes the censorship that American women who are writing as mothers impose on themselves and one another:

> . . . Well, at readings people are always tsk-tsking, although
> mothers are also nodding and sometimes crying but at least
> one person
> from every audience comes up to me and says, *you'll pay for
> that. Someday,*
> *he'll grow up and read that and you'll pay.*[5]

The cheeky decision to include this criticism in her book allows her to own it and to overcome it. The next lines of this poem go on to describe a new book about motherhood that she is currently writing.

In America, Zucker must also demonstrate that poetry about motherhood can actually be socially and politically relevant. In her long poem "Hey Allen Ginsberg Where Have You Gone and What Would You Think of My Drugs?," Zucker points out the shortcomings of framing national narratives through terms set up by childless males. Her poem's power and relevance come from the fact that the speaker is a mother of three Jewish sons, and, as she worries that taking antianxiety medication will shut down the "refugee gene" that got her Jewish family out of Europe in the nick of time, her children connect her to generations of refugees that came before her and the ones that are likely to follow. When she speaks as a mother, she is speaking as a nation, though not necessarily as a member of the nation, America, in which she now finds herself. No matter how reluctantly, she is (also) speaking as a mother within the Jewish nation.[6]

In Israel, such posturing is not necessary. Motherhood, both metaphorically and literally depicted, has long been deemed an appropriate expression of nationalism.[7] Indeed, the earliest depiction of the Israelites/Hebrews as a nation occurs when three angels prophesy that Sarah will give birth to a son.[8] And the continuation of the Hebrew nation in Egypt, and their exodus and subsequent settling in Canaan, is only possible after the Israelite women seduce men into annulling their vow not to produce children, which was made in response to Pharaoh's mandate that midwives must kill male Israelite babies.[9] Indeed, the drive to motherhood is justification for breaking patriarchal laws; it has been portrayed in Biblical literature as justification for incest, in the case of Lot's daughters, and prostitution, in the case of Judah's daughter-in-law, as well as for turning away insubordinate servants who happen to have borne children to one's husband, in the case of Sarah and Hagar.

Thus, in contemporary times, while childless Israeli female writers, such as Leah Goldberg, might be criticized for focusing on "personal emotion" rather than "important" world events, Gidali, writing about motherhood, does not suffer this fate. Nor does Gidali suffer from the kind of censorship imposed by cultural taste that others have suffered.

Israeli society is, of course, judgmental about suicide. The general feeling is that life goes on, and you do, too. Feelings are extravagances that are ill afforded during a time of crisis, such as war. Israeli mothers are not required to be happy as, perhaps, American mothers are. They are required to stay alive, no matter the external and mitigating circumstances. And Gidali falls in line here: she, too, is critical of suicide. Her motherhood poetry is not considered subversive. It is, in fact, an extremely faithful representation of what we imagine Israeli motherhood to be, which is why it is a valuable read.

But Gidali's surface adherence to the norms of Israeli motherhood and women's role in Israeli society, like her poetry's seemingly uncomplicated vocabulary and syntax, is misleading. Many of her constant references to Biblical depictions of motherhood, when examined closely, focus on the first moments of the ancient Arab-Israeli conflict through the figures of Jacob, Esau, Isaac, and Ishmael. The Biblical passages from which Gidali draws suggest that the mothers were instrumental in determining which sons were preferred; thus, they are responsible for shaping national identity. In contrast to them, as a modern mother, Gidali's poetic persona is ready to love her children equally. It might be that Gidali's poetry allows us to imagine a way of being in the world that does not yet exist.

In the poem "Boy, there is peat from under the swamp," Esau, the father of Israel's historic enemies, the Edomites, the Kenizzites, and the Amalekites, is welcomed back into the family, among the other Jewish brothers and sons who were lied to and tricked by their family members.[10] These include Joseph, who was sold by his brothers, and Jacob, who was given the wrong bride. Don't cry, says the poem, but rather

> Turn to God, my son, turn to some god and you will be redeemed within all this "our ancestors," and this "our children," and all the mediations, which again and again deceive.

These lines are placed in a footnote in the poem, as if they themselves were the "peat from under the swamp." Indeed, more of the poem is footnote than text, implying that the story on the surface, the story told by men and winners, is hardly the story at all. And, when one reads the passage of Genesis to which this poem refers, one notes that only after Esau has forgiven Jacob does God again affirm Jacob's status as a nation, changing Jacob's name to Israel.[11]

Similarly, "Heir to the Curfew" depicts a young mother

already dreading her infant son's military service. She muses:

> This week you learned to walk. Soon you will be able to climb Mount Moriah, your brother Ishmael at your side, and which of you will continue to the ascent, now that there is no one but you to offer a ram in your place.

In the Quran, it is Ishmael, not Isaac, who ascends Mount Moriah with Abraham. Without signaling through syntax or subject matter that the poems are about to introduce and normalize a new reality, this is precisely what they do. They succeed, they sound convincing, because they employ the ancient tropes of woman as mother and nation builder with which Hebrew-language audiences are well acquainted. But this nation builder, this mother, is implying that she is the mother of both children of the conflict. God will not intervene this time. Thus does Gidali liberate the future for a new kind of narrative, one with the possibility of cooperation and coexistence based on the suggestion of an original cooperation and coexistence.

Indeed, this argument is consistent throughout her three collections. Her first, pre-motherhood collection, *Twenty Girls to Envy Me* (2003)—from which this bilingual collection takes its name—opens with the poem "Did You Pack It Yourself?," which transforms the vaguely terrifying Israeli airport security check experience into an open-minded affirmation of the life impulse:

> Of all the questions
> to ask: Did you pack it yourself?
> Yes, by myself.
> It was hard, I said,
> but it is harder to fear that it will never come.
> I am not beautiful, you see,
> and the heart is the size of a fist.

Israel's national airline is the only major airline never to have been successfully hijacked, but Gidali hijacks the institution's meaning. Not by resisting the danger—the poem does answer the intended question—but by turning toward a life-affirming quest for community and connection. *Levad*, in Hebrew, has two meanings. The airport security question takes *levad* to mean "by yourself," but the speaker answers to the secondary meaning of the word, "unpartnered."

Thus, in seeking relationship, in seeking a partner, the poem affirms life in the face of difficult odds. The heart *is* like a fist. And the country *is* surrounded by other countries that wish, sometimes actively, that it did not exist. But a fist can be opened to hold another hand, and here is where life happens, in all of its outrageous, outraged, and tender vulnerability. And here is where language happens—creating the world it inhabits through a simple change in focus. In addition to answering a question intended to exclude a suspicious passenger from boarding a plane, the speaker answers a question about her availability and desire to welcome someone on board her life. Thus do the poem and the collection demonstrate that even the most intimate of relationships depend upon and are crafted and scripted by the external world, by language, ethics, and political realities.

Gidali's second book, *Closing In* (2009), is structured around the challenges of raising children and a stepchild in the space between a first wife's self-inflicted death and the children's future military service. This complements the subtext of Genesis that Gidali draws into the poetry. The speaker of Gidali's poetry is not like Sarah—she accepts the firstborn of another woman. Through this acceptance, this book examines the difficult negotiation of boundaries—between past and present, the self and others, the sacred and the secular, nation and nation.

To live in Gidali's Israel is to undergo a daily experiment

in low-grade negative capability, never knowing with absolute certainty that the country will be there the next day, and if so, where its boundaries will lie. Witness the opening poem from *Cradle*, "I Call to Tell a Friend that My Mother Is Dying." Here the speaker has found love and partnership, and has welcomed children into her life many times over. Still, she has not overcome the existential national angst, and is, therefore, unable to buy an apartment:

> I moved apartments three times in three years—it still
> beats buying, in my opinion. Who knows how long this
>   country will last.
>
> The children, the work, there's never enough time,
> I just called to hear your voice.
>
> Awful things going on in the world.
> How are you?

As in all of Gidali's work, the overwhelming conclusion (death, in this case) remains unstated, so as to make room for the details of everyday life. In return, the ordinary details of everyday life glow with extraordinary significance and beauty. They become microcosms of the unutterable forces at which we hurl names in an attempt at order.

In a country that is never out of the international spotlight—or the gaze of a deceased mother or a Biblical patriarch—one must strive to continue one's daily life in as normal a manner as possible. The tension between public display and private feeling is a constant in the daily life of any Israeli; thus Gidali's work is a negotiation between the myth and the individual who has inherited the myth.

This bilingual volume presents selections from Orit Gidali's three collections that I have described above: the 2003 *Twenty Girls to Envy Me*, which was performed at the

2006 Akko Theater Festival; *Closing In*, which was awarded a Rabinovitch Art Foundation prize and published in 2009; and *Cradle*, published in late 2015. Also included are two new poems, which, when I began this translation project, were intended for *Cradle*, but as *Cradle* became increasingly engaged in the work of mourning a mother, the poems were removed in anticipation of a fourth, linked book. We did include these two poems here, because I see them as bridge poems between *Closing In* and *Cradle*. In selecting the poems, I was guided by two considerations: quality and novelty. I sought poems that introduce previously unseen landscapes and situations—because distinctly "Israeli"—into English-language poetry. But even universal landscapes become novel in a Gidali poem, for Gidali has a mind that receives the world as if it had been created anew each day, in all its chaotic possibility. In this world, language is generative as well as denotative, and the past, present, and future are fluid, so that events and their heroes wander from one temporality to another; objects and characters leap from book to book.

I invited Gidali to help me select the poems, a process that gave her an opportunity to revise some of her work in the original Hebrew, and I translated the revisions into English. Gidali's revisions were of three kinds. The first was a simple insertion of punctuation marks and a reconsideration of line breaks. This was mainly confined to the earliest collection, *Twenty Girls to Envy Me*, which, Gidali felt, was not as attentive to punctuation as it might have been.

The second level of revision excised weaker stanzas from otherwise powerful poems; this occurred in "Songs to a Dead Woman" and "Etrog." The third type of revision was recombination. Twice we decided that the essence of a poem was actually contained in a single stanza, and, since many of the poems in each collection had been written in the same time period, Gidali felt that the salvaged stanza fit better into a different, but related poem. Thus, "My Beloved" ends with the stanza that originally belonged in the poem "Transparent Stitches," whose last line contains the phrase that is the title of the first book, "Twenty Girls to Envy Me." Aside from this salvaged stanza, we did not include "Transparent Stitches" in this bilingual edition. The second remixed poem is "The Love, Yonatan"; the current section 6 was originally section D of the poem "Like Rams," which is not included in this edition.

In translating Orit Gidali's work, I have tried to capture the initial impression of the poem in the original Hebrew, its cultural and linguistic complexity cloaked in simplicity. The poems do appear quite simple in Hebrew upon first read, because the vocabulary is ordinary. Most of the poems are composed of simple declarative sentences; the most common parts of speech are nouns and verbs. Their art lies in the fact that the key nouns and verbs contain multiple meanings, and the poems can be read in multiple ways. Because English has a larger vocabulary than Hebrew does, my challenge was to find equivalent syntax in English. Sometimes, as in the poem "Did You Pack It Yourself?," I had to introduce a preposition to achieve the double meaning. Thus, the question "did you pack it yourself" is answered "yes, *by* myself," in English. At other times, concepts that were new in Hebrew were not new in English, and to achieve the sense of newness, I had to disrupt the syntax of English, such as in the last two lines of "Reverse Sati."

For the sake of musicality and narrative pacing, I do not pause to explain words or concepts that may be unfamiliar to non-Israeli or non-Jewish readers, but I have provided a notes section at the end of the book for words, songs, cultural references, and Biblical passages, when relevant. These are personal poems, but never selfish ones. The poems exercise restraint in order to make a space for the reader; at the same time they are candid. As a translator, I strive to honor this restraint by refraining from being too interpretive in my translations, so as to make a space for the reader, as Orit Gidali does.

Marcela Sulak
September 2014, Tel Aviv

Notes

1. Yehuda Amichai, "All the Generations Before Me," trans. Harold Schimmel, in *Poems of Jerusalem and Love Poems* (Riverdale-on-Hudson, New York: Sheep Meadow Press, 1994), 2–3.
2. Unpublished email correspondence, September 11, 2014.
3. Yitzhak Laor, "Shirim Hakodoshim," *Ha'aretz*, June 7, 2009.
4. See, for example, Avi Garfinkel, "Milim le'akhuz bahen kmo me'aka," *Sefer b'shavua*, March 14, 2009, http://avigarfinkel.word press.com/2009/03/14; and Eli Hirsh's review of *Closing In*: Eli Hirsh, "Orit Gidali *Smichut*," *Yediot Ahronot*, March 6, 2009, http://elihirsh .com/?p=382.
5. Rachel Zucker, "Paying Down the Debt: Happiness," *Museum of Accidents* (Seattle: Wave Books, 2009), 46–51.
6. Ibid., 18–26.
7. Rachel S. Harris claims, in fact, that in cultural representations, an Israeli woman's national obligation lies exclusively in child production and child rearing (literally or metaphorically). See chapter 5, "Nothing Left to Live for" in her book *An Ideological Death: Suicide in Israeli Literature* (Evanston, IL: Northwestern University Press, 2014).
8. Genesis 15:1–4; Genesis 17:17–19; Genesis 18:9–14. In Genesis 20:17 and Genesis 21:1–7, God even punishes the household of Abimelek with childlessness, because he has taken Sarah from Abraham, thereby delaying her nation-building childbirth venture.
9. See Midrash Tanchuma and Rashi's commentary on Exodus 38:8, which describes how the women would overcome their husbands' fatigue and reluctance to conceive children through the use of a fish meal, wine, and mirrors. Rashi claims that God approved the feminine use of mirrors and, over the objections of Moses, allowed the women to donate them to decorate the Tabernacle: "The Holy One, Blessed is He, said: Accept them, because these are the dearest to Me of all, for

by means of them, the women established many legions of offspring in Egypt." This translation is from the *Artscroll Chumash*.

10. For the story of Esau and Jacob, see Genesis 27:1–40; for Jacob, Leah, and Rachel, see Genesis 29:1–30; for Joseph and his brothers, Genesis 37:1–35.

11. Genesis 32–33.

TRANSLATOR'S ACKNOWLEDGMENTS

The translator gratefully acknowledges the journals in which the following translations have previously appeared:

The Ilanot Reivew: "We Could Have Lived So Well, You Say, and Gaze at Her, Still Pretty," "Did You Pack It Yourself?," and "That Girl"

Blue Lyra: "Note" and "My Beloved"

Eleven Eleven: "Psalm," "God of Straw Mothers," and "A Thousand Nights"

Modern Poetry in Translation: "I Call to Tell a Friend that My Mother Is Dying"

The Bakery: "Transparent Stitches," from which the last stanza of the poem "My Beloved" comes, in this edition, "Kohelet," and "Hard Morning"

Poetry International website: "Kohelet," "Hard Morning," "Songs to a Dead Woman," "We Could Have Lived So Well, You Say, and Gaze at Her, Still Pretty," and "Soon It Will Be Dark"

The translator thanks Guy Sharett, her Hebrew tutor extraordinaire and consultant; Joanna Chen, who helped select the poems; Maya Klein, for her invaluable reading; Maya Lavie-Ajayi, for introducing her to Orit Gidali and Gidali's work; Sharron Hass, for her patient and radiant advice and support; and Wendy Moore at the Center for Middle Eastern Studies at the University of Texas.

FROM
Twenty Girls to Envy Me

DID YOU PACK IT YOURSELF?

Of all the questions
to ask: Did you pack it yourself?
Yes, by myself.
It was hard, I said,
but it is harder to fear that it will never come.
I am not beautiful, you see,
and the heart is the size of a fist.

ארזת לבד

מִכָּל הַשְּׁאֵלוֹת
לִשְׁאֹל: אָרַזְתְּ לְבַד?
כֵּן, לְבַד.
הָיָה קָשֶׁה, אָמַרְתִּי
אֲבָל יוֹתֵר קָשֶׁה לְפַחַד שֶׁזֶּה
לֹא יָבוֹא כְּבָר אַף פַּעַם.
אֵינֶנִּי יָפָה, אַתָּה מֵבִין,
וְהַלֵּב הוּא בְּגֹדֶל אֶגְרוֹף.

MY BELOVED

Filled were my days with suns.
Filled were my days with love.
When he comes to the door I will open to him
and I will be wet loam.

The balcony of my body is rosemary
and he, clusters of vines.
Sometimes in the darkness before he sleeps,
I hear a grape opening.

Behold, he arrives at the gate,
he removes the breastplate of his clothing
set with shards from the floor of our house.

He kisses me and permits me
to lay my ribs
in the space between his ribs
and I return to him.

*

He poeticizes our sated bodies
within earshot of his friends.
They listen and are burned
as by the imagined taste of lemon.

Then he waves good-bye.
The movement of his hand caresses from afar
all the organs of my body.

אהובי

מָלְאוּ יָמַי שְׁמָשׁוֹת
מָלְאוּ יָמַי אַהֲבָה
כְּשֶׁיָּבוֹא אֶפְתַּח אֶת הַדֶּלֶת
וְאֶהְיֶה אֲדָמָה רְטֻבָּה.

מְרַפֶּסֶת גּוּפִי לִקְרָאתוֹ רוֹזְמָרִין
וְהוּא אֶשְׁכּוֹלוֹת גְּפָנִים.
יֵשׁ, בַּחֹשֶׁךְ, בְּטֶרֶם שְׁנָתוֹ,
אֲנִי שׁוֹמַעַת עֵנָב נִפְתָּח.

הִנֵּה הוּא מַגִּיעַ לַשַּׁעַר,
מֵסִיר אֶת חֹשֶׁן בִּגְדוֹ
הַמְשֻׁבָּץ רְסִיסִים מֵרַצְפַת בֵּיתֵנוּ.

הוּא נוֹשֵׁק וּמַתִּיר לִי
לִפְרֹשׂ צַלְעוֹתַי
בַּמֶּרְוָח שֶׁבֵּין צַלְעוֹתָיו.
אֲנִי שָׁבָה אֵלָיו.

*

אֲהוּבִי מְשׁוֹרֵר בְּאָזְנֵי יְדִידִים
עַל שִׂמְחַת מֶחֱוַת גּוּפֵינוּ.
הֵם שׁוֹמְעִים וְנִכְוִים,
כְּאָדָם הַמְדַמְיֵן טַעֲמוֹ שֶׁל לִימוֹן.

כְּשֶׁעוֹצֵר מִדַּבְּרוֹ, מְבָרֵךְ לְשָׁלוֹם.
נִפְנוּף יָדוֹ מְלַטֵּף מֵרָחוֹק
אֶת כָּל אֵיבְרֵי גּוּפִי.

*

He kisses my hand,
my fingers extended like eyelashes.
He is a man holding an etrog,
bringing his nose close to smell it.

My beloved found a woman,
he sought and found her in himself.
She is beautiful. She is more beautiful than I.

*

My beloved is holding the sheet
as if it were the mold of my body.
If I wanted to explain it
I would have to twist my back.

(Even if I wrote about him for seven years,
the seven bad years wouldn't come.)

My beloved is spread before me,
his head within the frame of the pillow.
If I had money I would hire
twenty girls to envy me.

אֲהוּבִי מְנַשֵּׁק אֶת יָדִי הַנִּפְרֶשֶׂת
כְּמוֹ חִבּוּר הָרִיסִים אֶל עַפְעַף.
הוּא אָדָם הָאוֹחֵז אֶתְרוֹג
וּמְקָרֵב אַפּוֹ לְהָרִיחַ.

אֲהוּבִי שֶׁמָּצָא אִשָּׁה,
חִפֵּשׂ וּמָצָא בְּתוֹכוֹ.
הִיא יָפָה, הִיא יָפָה מִמֶּנִּי.

*

אֲהוּבִי אוֹחֵז בַּסָּדִין
כְּמוֹ הָיָה תַּבְנִית גּוּפִי.
אִם אֶרְצֶה לְהַסְבִּיר אוֹתוֹ
אֶצְטָרֵךְ לְפַתֵּל אֶת גַּבִּי.

(גַּם אִם אֶכְתֹּב עָלָיו שֶׁבַע שָׁנִים,
לֹא יָבוֹאוּ הַשָּׁנִים הָרָעוֹת.)

אֲהוּבִי פָּרוּשׂ מוּלִי
רֹאשׁוֹ בְּמִסְגֶּרֶת הַכַּר.
לוּ הָיָה לִי כֶּסֶף הָיִיתִי שׂוֹכֶרֶת
עֶשְׂרִים נְעָרוֹת לְקַנֵּא.

NOTE

My beloved wakes up,
my body warm on him.
Meat mixes with milk.

פתק

אֲהוּבִי מִתְעוֹרֵר,
גּוּפִי חַם מֵעָלָיו,
בָּשָׂר מִתְעַרְבֵּב בֶּחָלָב.

HARD MORNING

It was a difficult morning for us, the light wasn't kind,
all at once I looked fat, I preferred to shower alone,
you got ready in the bedroom, put on a white shirt,
the one, I think, in which you were married the first time,
and the night continued to clot into morning,
the tone of my voice when I pushed you: "I can't, not now,"
and you slowly circling, not saying a word, and how
is it that I remember my Hungarian uncle Earl shouting
    "puszi, puszi, girl."
Be'er Sheva, I was small, his shirt had filled
with sweat when he ran after the car to ask me for a kiss,
in fact, he wore a tank top, but what would this precision
    recover,
he shouted *"puszi, puszi,* girl," that is what you should know,
he shouted "pussy, pussy, girl."

בוקר קשה

הָיָה לָנוּ בֹּקֶר קָשֶׁה, הָאוֹר לֹא הֵיטִיב אִתָּנוּ,
נִרְאֵיתִי פִּתְאֹם שְׁמֵנָה, הֶעֱדַפְתִּי מִקְלַחַת לְבַד,
אַתָּה הִסְתַּדַּרְתָּ בַּחֶדֶר, לָבַשְׁתָּ חֻלְצָה לְבָנָה
שֶׁנִּדְמֶה לִי שֶׁבָּהּ הִתְחַתַּנְתָּ בַּפַּעַם הָרִאשׁוֹנָה,
וְהַלַּיְלָה הַמְשִׁיךְ לִנְזֹל, גּוּשִׁים אֶל תּוֹךְ הַבֹּקֶר,
גּוֹן קוֹלִי כְּשֶׁדָּחַפְתִּי אוֹתְךָ: "לֹא עַכְשָׁו, אֲנִי לֹא יְכוֹלָה"
וְאַתָּה הַסּוֹבֵב לְאַט, לֹא אוֹמֵר לִי מִלָּה, אֵיךְ
קָרָה שֶׁנִּזְכַּרְתִּי בְּאָרוֹל צוֹעֵק "פּוּסִי, פּוּסִי, יַלְדָּה."
בְּאֵר-שֶׁבַע, הָיִיתִי קְטַנָּה, חֻלְצָתוֹ הִתְמַלְּאָה
מִזֵּעָה כְּשֶׁהוּא רָץ אַחֲרֵי הַמְּכוֹנִית לְבַקֵּשׁ נְשִׁיקָה
מִמֶּנִּי, בְּעֶצֶם לָבַשׁ גּוּפִיָּה, אֲבָל מַה כְּבָר יַצִּיל הַדִּיּוּק
הוּא צָעַק "פּוּסִי, פּוּסִי, יַלְדָּה", זֶה מַה שֶּׁחָשׁוּב שֶׁתֵּדַע
הוּא צָעַק פּוּסִי פּוּסִי יַלְדָּה.

PSALM

My eardrum plays in your honor a psalm of waking up for
    money, a psalm of victors filling up with fuel, victors on
    their way, victors queuing at the cash register.
Light switches straight as erections—stop dreaming, stop
    dreaming—I shove at you something I threw together
    for you to take
to work, you're a baby at efficiency mumbling *thank you.*
    Be careful there in the boulevard, which you can see
    from the office window,
its trees were planted intentionally, they didn't grow by
    themselves. Be careful in the noise, which is rising up to
    attack you with a lack of temperance,
don't be seduced by the seraphim of more.

I promised we would make iron of this day, and then we
    would refuse to use it, who am I kidding, wake up, wake
    up, the work
of the world beating warm at our door. If you return in a
    full suitcase, then we will embrace, a halo held by a halo;
if not full, we will embrace, one holding the other, an
    anxious hello.

הילה אחוזה בהילה

תֹּף אָזְנִי מְנַגֵּן לִכְבוֹדְךָ מִזְמוֹר לַקָּמִים לַכֶּסֶף, מִזְמוֹר לַמְנַצְּחִים בַּדֶּלֶק, בַּדֶּרֶךְ, בַּתּוֹר
לַקֻּפּוֹת,

מִפְּסְקֵי הַחַשְׁמַל יְשָׁרִים כְּזִקְפָּה, אַל תַּחְלֹם, אַל תַּחְלֹם, אֲנִי דּוֹחֶפֶת לְךָ מַשֶּׁהוּ
שֶׁהֵכַנְתִּי שֶׁתִּתְקַח

לַעֲבוֹדָה, אַתָּה תִּינוֹק-לְעָבֵר-הַיְּעִילוּת מְמַלְמֵל תּוֹדָה, הִזָּהֵר לְךָ שָׁם בַּשְּׂדֵרָה
שֶׁרוֹאִים מֵחַלּוֹן הַמִּשְׂרָד,

עֲצִיָּה נִטְעוּ בְכַוָּנָה לֹא גָדְלוּ מֵעַצְמָם, הִזָּהֵר מֵהָרַעַשׁ הַקָּם לְהַתְקִיפְךָ בְּחֹסֶר מִדָּה
טוֹבָה

אַל תֵּלֵךְ אֶל שַׂרְפֵי-הַעֹד.

הַבְטָחְתִּי שֶׁנַּעֲשָׂה מֵהַיּוֹם הַזֶּה בַּרְזֶל וּנְסָרֵב לְהִשְׁתַּמֵּשׁ בּוֹ, אֶת מִי אֲנִי מְרַמָּה, קוּם,
קוּם, עֲבוֹדַת

הָעוֹלָם עַל הַדֶּלֶת מַכָּה וְחַמָּה, אִם תַּחְזֹר בְּמִזְוָדָה מְלֵאָה נִתְחַבֵּק, הִלָּה אֲחוּזָה
בְּהִלָּה,

אִם לֹא מְלֵאָה נִתְחַבֵּק, שְׁנֵי אֲנָשִׁים אֲחוּזִים זֶה בַּזֶּה, אֲחֻזָּה בֵּינֵיהֶם בְּהָלָה.

THE BINDING OF ISAAC V

And what still binds me to the hard faces,
the veiled faces, to this wandering
without wings in the land of heat?
Maybe it's Abraham in a convenience store saying,
"Just give me a ten, and we'll call it even,"
generosity building a cool pool in him—
it was a very hot day—I entered to bathe.
Maybe he's the one standing between me and the map,
blocking its length, its narrowness rife
with terror, a country the shape of a knife.

עקדה V

וּמַה מַּצְמִית אוֹתִי עֲדַיִן לַפָּנִים הַקָּשׁוֹת,
לְרָעוּלֵי הַפָּנִים הַקָּשׁוֹת, לַנְּדִידָה
בְּלִי כְּנָפַיִם בְּאֶרֶץ הַחֹם?
אוּלַי אַבְרָם מֵהַמַּכֵּלֶת שֶׁאָמַר: "שֶׁיִּהְיֶה
בַּעֲשָׂרָה" וְהַנְּדִיבוּת בָּנְתָה בְּתוֹכוֹ
בְּרֵכָה קְרִירָה, הָיָה
יוֹם שָׁרָב, נִכְנַסְתִּי לִרְחֹץ בְּתוֹכָהּ -
אוּלַי זֶה הוּא שֶׁעוֹמֵד בֵּינִי לְבֵין הַמַּפָּה
מַסְתִּיר אֶת אָרְכָּהּ, צָרְוּתָהּ הַמְּבֹהֶלֶת:
מְדִינָה בְּצוּרַת מַאֲכֶלֶת.

THAT GIRL

I am the girl who is more afraid of recess
than the lesson. It's not clear
what you need to do. Other children—
missed opportunities.

*

Sitting up straight and pointing a finger
at the ceiling's face—
adults, adults,
come and collect this tall hand,
draw it from childhood.

*

By the rungs of the years I seek to arise from her,
to try not to try too hard,
to try to put things carelessly,
to reinforce the foundation of the bedroom.

When her finger reaches my foot, I will be disillusioned,
the whole earth is filled with the weight of it.

ילדה

אֲנִי הַיַּלְדָּה הַפְּסָקָה מַפְחִידָה אוֹתִי
יוֹתֵר מִן הַשִּׁעוּר לֹא בָּרוּר
מַה צָּרִיךְ לַעֲשׂוֹת, יְלָדִים אֲחֵרִים
הֶחָמִצוֹת.

*

מַצְבִּיעָה בִּזְקִיפוּת קוֹמָה הָאֶצְבַּע
נִשְׁלַחַת אֶל פְּנֵי הַתִּקְרָה
מְבֻגָּרִים, מְבֻגָּרִים
בּוֹאוּ וְאִסְפוּ אֶת הַיָּד הַגְּבוֹהָה
מְשׁוּ אוֹתָהּ מִן הַיַּלְדוּת.

*

בְּחֻקַּי - הַשָּׁנִים אֲבַקֵּשׁ לַעֲלוֹת מִמֶּנָּה,
לֹא לָצֵאת מִגְּדֵרִי,
לְהָנִיחַ דְּבָרִים בְּרִשּׁוּל,
לִסְמֹךְ בְּאִשּׁוּשִׁים אֶת חֲדַר הַשֵּׁנָה.

כְּשֶׁתִּתְפֹּס אֶצְבָּעָהּ אֶת רַגְלִי אֶתְבַּדֵּהּ.
כָּל הָאָרֶץ כְּבֵדָה.

SARAH LAUGHED AGAIN

When father raised his hands you laughed
like crazy till the whole mountain bristled
with goose bumps.
Rams whispered to fawns
to stay close.
The whole mountain crazy
calling me by name,
begging to hear me
just this once
laughing back at you.
The knife falls and one more knife,
my father like a magician before a box—
he's not cutting for real.
Your two hands spread in supplication—
how will I explain it to you?—
the laughter didn't come from me.

שרה

כְּשֶׁאַבָּא הֵרִים יָדַיִם, אַתְּ צָחַקְתְּ
כְּמוֹ מְטֹרֶפֶת, כָּל הָהָר הִסְתַּמֵּר.
אֵילִים לָחֲשׁוּ לָעֳפָרִים
שֶׁיִּשָּׁאֲרוּ קָרוֹב.
כָּל הָהָר, מְטֹרֶפֶת,
קוֹרֵאת לִי בִּשְׁמִי,
מִתְחַנֶּנֶת לִשְׁמֹעַ אוֹתִי
רַק הַפַּעַם
צוֹחֵק חֲזָרָה בִּשְׁבִילֵךְ.
מַאֲכֶלֶת יוֹרֶדֶת וְעוֹד מַאֲכֶלֶת
אַבָּא שֶׁלִּי כְּמוֹ קוֹסֵם מוּל תֵּבָה
לֹא חוֹתֵךְ בֶּאֱמֶת.
אַתְּ עוֹמֶדֶת מוּלוֹ,
שְׁתֵּי יָדַיִךְ פּוֹרֶשֶׂת
אֵיךְ אַסְבִּיר לָךְ אֶת זֶה,
לֹא יָצָא לִי הַצְּחוֹק.

KOHELET

I, Kohelet, was king of Jerusalem.
I really was.
Treading a thousand flowers en route to the white bed
where my wives awaited to remove from my head
the crown made of marzipan, biting it and with sweet
   tongues,
my silk rubbing against their silk, my flesh would choose
among them, already sweet in their flesh.

Kohelet, I held a thousand women,
and I didn't have a single one
I could recognize by smell
or by her skin or her feet,
her steps as she walked away from me: David's lament.
Her steps toward me: his song.

I am Kohelet, Solomon,
my linen, the mystery of shrouds,
and my bitten crown is above me.

קוהלת

אֲנִי קֹהֶלֶת מֶלֶךְ הָיִיתִי בִּירוּשָׁלַיִם
בֶּאֱמֶת הָיִיתִי
דּוֹרֵךְ עַל אֶלֶף פְּרָחִים בְּדַרְכִּי לַמִּטָּה הַלְּבָנָה
שָׁם חִכּוּ נְשׁוֹתַי, שֶׁהֵסִירוּ אֶת כֶּתֶר רֹאשִׁי
הֶעָשׂוּי מַרְצִיפָּן בִּנְגִיסַת לְשׁוֹנוֹת מְתוּקוֹת, מְשִׁיִּי
מִתְחַכֵּךְ בְּמִשְׁיָן, וְהָיִיתִי בּוֹחֵר מְתוּכָן לִבְשָׂרִי,
וּבְשָׂרִי כְּבָר מָתוֹק בִּבְשָׂרָן.

קֹהֶלֶת הֶחֱזַקְתִּי אֶלֶף נָשִׁים
וְלֹא הָיְתָה לִי אִשָּׁה יְחִידָה
לְזַהוֹת אֶת רֵיחָהּ
וְעוֹרָהּ וְרַגְלֶיהָ
צְעָדֶיהָ מִמֶּנִּי: קִינַת דָּוִד
צְעָדֶיהָ אֵלַי: שִׁירָתוֹ

אֲנִי קֹהֶלֶת שְׁלֹמֹה
סִתְרֵי תַּכְרִיכִים שֶׁל סְדִינַי
וְכִתְרֵי הַנָּגוֹס מֵעָלַי.

ISAAC

1.

Now at last, Isaac, you stand before your father's bed,
bending over it, documenting nonstop,
there is a looseness of bowels and bladder.

Once you were two strangers, but this condition
is the saliva on a stamp sent to you both—
with one blow he tried to cut down your life,
and now his life falls trickling down.

2.

The breath that in the end waits only to blow
is short of ordinary words,
it will soon be spread into Shabbat, it won't reach the end
of next week. Stand by till then.

Your erect penis
from which the tent of your body falls,
your silent sperm accumulates in the world, filling it up.
For now, it's him; afterward, it's just you.

3.

Help him, now they are serving him a tray,
then help him clean his dentures, too.
You shall imitate their movement, "Behold, here I am,"
dropping them into a glass.

יצחק

א.

וּבְכֵן סוֹף סוֹף אַתָּה יִצְחָק, לִפְנֵי מִטַּת אָבִיךָ,
רָכוּן מְתַעֵד בְּלִי הֶפְסֵק:
הִנֵּה רִפְיוֹן סוּגְרַיִם.

פַּעַם - הֱיִיתֶם שְׁנַיִם זָרִים אֲבָל הַרְטִיבוּת
הַזּוֹ כְּמוֹ רַק עַל בּוּלִים,
שָׁלְחָה אֶתְכֶם בְּיַחַד-
נִסָּה בְּמַכָּה אַחַת לְהוֹרִיד אֶת כָּל חַיֶּיךָ
וְשֶׁלּוֹ יוֹרְדִים עַכְשָׁו בְּטִפְטוּף.

ב.

מֵאַחַר לְדַבֵּר, הַנְּשִׁימָה שְׁרוֹצָה בְּסוֹפָהּ רַק לִנְשֹׁף
קְצָרָה בְּמִלִּים שֶׁל חֹל, עוֹד מְעַט נְסוּכָה בְּשַׁבָּת, לֹא תַּגִּיעַ אֶל סוֹף
הַשָּׁבוּעַ הַבָּא, בֵּינְתַיִם הָכֵן.

אֵיבָרֶיךָ הַזָּקוּר
מִסָּבִיב שָׁמֹט אֶת אֹהֶל גּוּפְךָ
זַרְעֲךָ הַשֶּׁקֶט יִצְטַבֵּר בָּעוֹלָם הַהוֹלֵךְ וְנִמְלָא
בֵּינְתַיִם זֶה הוּא אַחַר-כָּךְ רַק אַתָּה.

ג.

תַּעֲזֹר לוֹ עַכְשָׁו מַגִּישִׁים לוֹ מַגָּשׁ
אַחַר-כָּךְ תַּעֲזֹר גַּם לִרְחֹץ תּוֹתָבוֹת
תְּחַקֶּה תְּנוּעָתָן: "הִנְנִי" שָׁמֹט לַכּוֹס.

4.

Enough with the writing, already, Isaac,
the insult of redundancy, *Abraham, Abraham, Lech Lecha.*
His angels don't answer. Standing before a bed,
just you.

In a distant room, from the mountain peak,
a plain is filled with barrenness,
for example, collated sheets,
for example, "my father" on your tongue.

5.

Lech Lecha, Go Forth to your house:
he who is running toward you
will continue, a constant in time.
Ask to omit *the one whom thou lovest,*
from *thy son, thy only son.*

For now, it's him; afterward, it's awe.

ה.

דַּי לִכְתֹּב כְּבָר יִצְחָק דַּי לִכְתֹּב, לֶךְ־לְךָ
מֵעֶלְבּוֹן הַכְּפִילוּת "אַבְרָהָם, אַבְרָהָם", לֶךְ־לְךָ
מֵרֻבֵּי דְּבוּרְךָ בֵּינְתַיִם נוֹזֵל מִיַּלֵּל מַלְאָכָיו לֹא עוֹנִים
עוֹמֵד מוּל מִטָּה
רַק אַתָּה.

בְּחֶדֶר רָחוֹק מֵראשׁ הַר
מִישׁוֹר מִתְמַלֵּא טְרָשִׁים
לְמָשָׁל, סְדִינִים אֲסוּפִים
לְמָשָׁל, לְשׁוֹנְךָ שֶׁאוֹמֶרֶת אָבִי.

ה.

לֶךְ־לְךָ לְבֵיתְךָ מִי שֶׁרַץ לִקְרָאתְךָ
יַמְשִׁיךְ כְּקָבוּעַ בַּזְּמַן
בַּקֵּשׁ לְהַשְׁמִיט אֲהוּבְךָ
מִשֶּׁלְּךָ יְחִידְךָ, לְהָאִיר אֶת
הַדֶּרֶךְ צָרָה כְּתוֹלַעַת רָמָה.

בֵּינְתַיִם זֶה הוּא אַחַר־כָּךְ בְּעָתָה.

SAMSON AND ABSALOM

Samson and Absalom
are comparing hair,
whose is more torn.

Absalom talks about pain,
Samson undresses
and shows him it is empty inside.

Absalom embraces him.
Not a single bird falls.
Not a single bird departs.

שמשון ואבשלום

שִׁמְשׁוֹן וְאַבְשָׁלוֹם
מַשְׁוִים שְׂעָרוֹת
שֶׁל מִי יוֹתֵר קָרוּעַ.

אַבְשָׁלוֹם מְדַבֵּר עַל כְּאֵב,
שִׁמְשׁוֹן מִתְפַּשֵּׁט
וּמַרְאֶה לוֹ שֶׁרֵיק בִּפְנִים.

אַבְשָׁלוֹם מְחַבֵּק אוֹתוֹ.
שׁוּם צִפּוֹר לֹא נוֹפֶלֶת.
שׁוּם צִפּוֹר לֹא מַמְרִיאָה.

FROM
Closing In

FROM SONGS TO A DEAD WOMAN

You

1.

When you rose up in the elevator, you were not holding
    her in your arms.
When you stretched out in bed, you were not holding her
    in your arms.
When you opened the window, you were not holding her
    in your arms.
When you took the dizziness pills, you were not holding
    her in your arms.
When you stood on the windowsill, you were not holding
    her in your arms.

She lays in bed, your daughter. From time to time she cries
    out in her sleep.
People gather, bobbing their heads around her blanket,
bobbing like all her childhood seesaws, gathering
    against her.
Move over, children; let her go first.

You rose through floor after floor,
the umbilical cord adrift behind you
like the ribbon of a gift
that will never be given.

2.

Which belly did I come out of, your daughter is asking at
    bedtime,
where is this belly, what is it holding now.

מתוך: שירים לאישה מתה

את

.1

כְּשֶׁעָלִית בַּמַּעֲלִית לֹא הֶחֱזַקְתָּ אוֹתָהּ בְּיָדֶיךָ.
כְּשֶׁהִשְׁתָּרַעְתָּ עַל הַמִּטָּה לֹא הֶחֱזַקְתָּ אוֹתָהּ בְּיָדֶיךָ.
כְּשֶׁפָּתַחְתָּ אֶת הַחַלּוֹן וְהָרוּחַ נָשְׁבָה, לֹא הֶחֱזַקְתָּ אוֹתָהּ בְּיָדֶיךָ.
צִנָּה כָּזוֹ יְכוֹלָה לִגְרֹם שֶׁתִּצְטַנֵּן.
כְּשֶׁלָּקַחְתָּ אֶת כַּדּוּרֵי הַטִּשְׁטוּשׁ לֹא הֶחֱזַקְתָּ אוֹתָהּ בְּיָדֶיךָ.
כְּשֶׁנֶּעֱמַדְתָּ עַל הָאָרֶן לֹא לָקַחְתָּ אוֹתָהּ בְּיָדֶיךָ.

הִיא שָׁכְבָה בְּמִטָּתָהּ. מִדֵּי פַּעַם הִשְׁמִיעָה בְּכִי מִתּוֹךְ שֵׁנָה.
אֲנָשִׁים נֶאֶסְפוּ לָנוּד סְבִיב שְׁמִיכָתָהּ,
לָנוּד כְּמוֹ כָּל נַדְנֵדוֹת יַלְדוּתָהּ הַנֶּאֱסָפוֹת כְּנֶגְדָּהּ,
זוּזוּ יְלָדִים, תְּנוּ לָהּ שֶׁתִּהְיֶה רִאשׁוֹנָה.

קוֹמָה אַחֲרֵי קוֹמָה עָבַרְתְּ.
חֶבֶל הַטַּבּוּר רִחֵף אַחֲרַיִךְ
כְּמוֹ סֶרֶט שֶׁל מַתָּנָה
שֶׁלְּעוֹלָם לֹא תִּנָּתֵן.

.2

מֵאֵיזוֹ בֶּטֶן יָצָאתִי הִיא שׁוֹאֶלֶת לִפְנֵי הַשֵּׁנָה,
אֵיפֹה הַבֶּטֶן הַזּוֹ מַה הִיא עַכְשָׁו מַחֲזִיקָה.

Your Daughter

1.

Her black eyes remember how you went away and didn't
    come back
and you left only the color of the road in her pupils as a
    souvenir.

2.

Behold, who is this that cometh up from the kindergarten,
laying down her drawings in which I am not drawn.
She scatters the grains of rice on the plate to create a
    thin lace.
And she does not give a single word away.
May the air between us not be filled even for a moment.

From the window you can see the playground,
which is painted in primary colors,
colors simple and pretty,
so close to the house.

3.

Sometimes it seems as if closeness were possible,
as between two consonants of a word
written with diacritical marks.

But only the frame
catches the slamming door
in its two hands.
The handle straightens like a blank line.

ילדתך

.1

עֵינֶיהָ שְׁחוֹרוֹת.
זוֹכְרוֹת שֶׁנָּסַעְתְּ וְלֹא חָזַרְתְּ
וְהִשְׁאַרְתְּ רַק אֶת צֶבַע הַכְּבִישׁ
בְּאִישׁוֹנֶיהָ לְמַזְכֶּרֶת.

.2

הִנֵּה הִיא עוֹלָה מִן הַגַּן,
מַנִּיחָה אֶת הַצִּיּוּרִים שֶׁבָּהֶם אֵינִי מְצֻיֶּרֶת,
פּוֹרַעַת אֶת גַּרְגְּרֵי הָאֹרֶז הַיּוֹצְרִים רִקְמָה דַּקָּה עַל הַצַּלַּחַת.

וְאֵינָהּ מַסְגִּירָה לִי מִלָּה אַחַת.
שֶׁלֹּא יִתְמַלֵּא וְלוּ לְרֶגַע הָאֲוִיר הָעוֹמֵד בֵּינֵינוּ
כִּרְצוּעַת מָגֵן.

מִן הַחַלּוֹן נִבָּט מִגְרַשׁ הַמִּשְׂחָקִים
הַצָּבוּעַ צִבְעֵי בָּסִיס.
צְבָעִים פְּשׁוּטִים וְיָפִים
סְמוּכִים כָּל כָּךְ אֶל הַבַּיִת.

.3

לִפְעָמִים נִדְמֶה שֶׁהַקִּרְבָה אֶפְשָׁרִית
כְּמוֹ בֵּין שְׁתֵּי אוֹתִיּוֹת בְּמִלָּה
בִּכְתִיב חָסֵר.

אֲבָל רַק הַמַּשְׁקוֹף
אוֹסֵף בִּשְׁתֵּי יָדָיו אֶת הַדֶּלֶת
בְּעֵת הַטְּרִיקָה
וְהַיָּדִית מִתְיַשֶּׁרֶת כְּמוֹ שׁוּרָה רֵיקָה.

Your Husband

1.

Two boxes in the bedroom.
Photos of the first wedding above photos of the second.
In one he bends toward me or toward you.
His large hand is binding.

2.

The baby's first kick didn't excite him as a first kick.
His eyes lit up and went dark
like the blink of a silent siren.

3.

Sometimes in the morning your name is spoken,
rushing our speech so as not to tread on you by accident.
Most of the time you are lying there, quiet,
a room that hasn't been swept.

4.

Curse of Rachel and Leah burning in me,
this curse of she who does not know which of them is she.

בַּעְלֵךְ

1.

שְׁתֵּי הַקֻּפְסָאוֹת בַּחֲדַר הַשֵּׁנָה.
תְּמוּנוֹת הַחֲתֻנָּה הָרִאשׁוֹנָה מֵעַל תְּמוּנוֹת הַשְּׁנִיָּה.
בְּאַחַת הוּא רוֹכֵן לִקְרָאתִי אוֹ לִקְרָאתֵךְ,
יָדוֹ הַגְּדוֹלָה כּוֹרֶכֶת.

2.

בַּבְּעִיטָה הָרִאשׁוֹנָה שֶׁל הַיֶּלֶד
לֹא הִתְרַגֵּשׁ כְּמוֹ בִּבְעִיטָה רִאשׁוֹנָה.
הִדְלִיק אֶת עֵינָיו וְכִבָּה
כְּמוֹ סִירֶנָה שְׁקֵטָה מְהַבְהֶבֶת.

3.

יֵשׁ בְּקָרִים מְזֻדְּמֵן לָנוּ לוֹמַר אֶת שְׁמֵךְ.
אֲנַחְנוּ מַחְלִישִׂים בְּדִבּוּרֵנוּ שֶׁלֹּא לִדְרֹךְ עָלַיִךְ בְּטָעוּת.
רֹב הַזְּמַן אַתְּ שׁוֹכֶבֶת שָׁם שְׁקֵטָה,
חֶדֶר שֶׁלֹּא טָאטָא.

4.

קִלְלַת רָחֵל וְלֵאָה בּוֹעֶרֶת עַל לְשׁוֹנִי,
קִלְלַת זוֹ שֶׁאֵינָהּ יוֹדַעַת מִי מֵהֶן הִיא.

GOD OF STRAW MOTHERS

God of straw mothers who are prepared to burn because
    there is no real blood in them,
God of the sender-of-them into battle and into the living
    room arena and into the wreckage,
God who stands them in a place in which there are no
    bulletproof vests and no steel helmets and the tongue is
    the edge of a javelin that cannot be thrown far from the
    body and everything stands exposed before the horses of
    the daughter who is galloping on her words,
God of the distance between two bedrooms as between
    two fingers signaling victory,
God of defeat,
God of she who will not permit them to touch her,
God of hope, "Hatikva," which is sung like a private
    anthem,
God of the insult muttered under one's breath,
God of silence,

You who made mother from the rib can also create from
the extended hand I reach toward her all morning to
remove a stray hair or to caress her face in the course of
my movements and immediately retract my hand, afraid to
be proven wrong.

אלוהי אמהות הקש

אֱלֹהֵי אִמָּהוֹת הַקַּשׁ הַמּוּכָנוֹת לְהִשָּׂרֵף כִּי אֵין בֶּן דַּם אֱמֶת, רַק רֹק אֱמֶת וִידֵי אֱמֶת
וְהַלְמוּת־לֵב אֱמֶת. אֱלֹהֵי הַשּׁוֹלֵחַ אוֹתָן אֶל קֶרֶב הַבַּיִת וְזִירַת הַסָּלוֹן וּמִלְחֲמוֹת
הַשְּׁבָרִים. אֱלֹהֵי הַמַּעֲמִיד אוֹתָן בְּמָקוֹם שֶׁבּוֹ אֵין אֲפוֹדִים וְאֵין קַסְדוֹת פֶּלֶד, וְהַלָּשׁוֹן
הִיא קְצֵה חֲנִית שֶׁלֹּא נִתָּן לְהָטִיל הָרָחֵק מִן הַגּוּף, וְהַכֹּל עוֹמֵד חָשׂוּף אֶל מוּל סוּסֵי
הַבַּת הַדּוֹהֶרֶת בִּמְלוֹתֶיהָ, לִבְדֹּק מַה יַּעֲמֹד הַפַּעַם אַחֲרֵי שֶׁתְּהַלֵּם

אֱלֹהֵי הַמֶּרְחָק שֶׁבֵּין שְׁנֵי חַדְרֵי הַשֵּׁנָה, כְּמוֹ בֵּין שְׁתֵּי אֶצְבָּעוֹת הַמַּסְמְנוֹת נִצָּחוֹן,
אֱלֹהֵי הַתְּבוּסָה, אֱלֹהֵי זוֹ שֶׁלֹּא תִּתֵּן שֶׁיִּפְגְּעוּ בָּהּ כִּי פַּעַם נִגְּעָה, אֱלֹהֵי הַתִּקְוָה
שֶׁמּוּשֶׁרֶת כְּמוֹ הִמְנוֹן פְּרָטִי וְאָז כָּבָה, אֱלֹהֵי הָעֶלְבּוֹן הַמְדֻבָּר רַק פְּנִימָה, אֱלֹהֵי
הַשְּׁתִיקָה

אַתָּה שֶׁעָשִׂיתָ מִן הַצֵּלָע אִם עַל עֶצְבּוֹנָהּ, יָכוֹל לַעֲשׂוֹת גַּם מִן הַיָּד הַשְּׁלוּחָה, שֶׁאֲנִי
שׁוֹלַחַת אֶל פָּנֶיהָ כָּל בֹּקֶר כְּדֵי לְהָזִיז שַׂעֲרָה סוֹרֶרֶת אוֹ כְּדֵי לְלַטֵּף אַגַּב תְּנוּעָה,
וּמִיָּד מְשִׁיבָה וְנָסוֹגָה, פּוֹחֶדֶת שֶׁאֶתְבַּדֶּה.

WE COULD HAVE LIVED
SO WELL, YOU SAY, AND
GAZE AT HER, STILL PRETTY

In a little while Shabbat in the Sharon, and traffic lights
take off their red, and the laces unravel and yield the bare
foot, and the records of the word gather into a book and
rest from their anxiousness to break, and the change in the
wallet emphasizes the victory of the many and the small,
and the expiration dates on the milk do not threaten to be
expired, and the first fruits are relaxing in sealed bags, and
the ice in the freezer assumes the shape of the most self-
confident mold, and the Styrofoam separates into small
balls that do not need the practical, and the central air
does not apologize for deceiving the heat, and the screens
do not apologize for deceiving the brightness, and the
poetry switches off the linoleum floor and switches on the
ceiling,

and the adolescents are softer and are not putting off thank
you, and what is piling up is piling up, and what is split is
split, and the clouds ponder the field, and the field ponders
the fish that float among the bushes in their imagination,
and in the vineyards, grapes turn into raisins, others into
wine, and not all the sweet ones are contaminated with
maggots of worry, and he who asks for a deluge does not
intend annihilation, but only a hard, streaming rain, and
the community leaders return from the road, gathering
a family to themselves, and generosity is being seen as a
quiet virtue and not for display, and mistakes are removed
from the heart of things, and the body's exchanges are
just, and the public domain is full of permissions, and the
private domains are full,

יכולנו לחיות טוב כל כך, אתה אומר, ומביט בה, יפה עדיין

עוֹד מְעַט שַׁבָּת בַּשָּׁרוֹן וְהָרְמַזוֹרִים מִתְפַּשְּׁטִים מֵאָדָם, וְהַשְּׁרוֹכִים נִפְרָמִים
וּמְוַתְּרִים לְרֶגֶל הַיְחֵפָה, וְשִׂיאֵי הָעוֹלָם מִתְכַּנְּסִים בְּסֵפֶר וְנָחִים מִבֶּהָלָתָם לְשָׁבֹּ,
וְהָעֹדֶף שֶׁבָּאָרֶנְק מַדְגִּישׁ אֶת נִצְחוֹן הַהַרְבֵּה וְהַקָּטָן, וְתַאֲרִיכֵי הַתְּפוּגָה שֶׁעַל הֶחָלָב
לֹא מַאְמִים לְהִפָּגַע, וְהַבְּכוּרִים מִתְרַוְּחִים בַּשְּׁקִיּוֹת הָאָטוּמוֹת, וְהַקֶּרַח שֶׁבַּמַּקְפִּיא
מְקַבֵּל עַל עַצְמוֹ אֶת צוּרַת הַתַּבְנִית הַבְּטוּחָה בְּעַצְמָהּ, וְהַקְּלַקֶּר נִפְרָד לְכַדּוּרִים
קְטַנִּים שֶׁלֹּא זְקוּקִים לַשִּׁמּוּשִׁי, וְהַמַּזְגָּנִים לֹא מִתְנַצְּלִים עַל שֶׁהֵם מְזַיְּפִים אֶת הַחֹם,
וְהַמָּסַכִּים לֹא מִתְנַצְּלִים עַל שֶׁהֵם מְזַיְּפִים אֶת הַנְּהָרָה, וְהַשִּׁירָה מְכַבָּה אֶת רִצְפַּת
הַלִּינוֹלִיאוּם וּמַדְלִיקָה אֶת הַתִּקְרָה,

וְהַמִּתְבַּגְּרִים רַכִּים יוֹתֵר וְלֹא מְלִינִים אֶת הַתּוֹדָה, וּמַה שֶּׁמִּתְחַשֵּׁר מִתְחַשֵּׁר אֲבָל
מַה שֶּׁנִּבְקַע נִבְקַע, וּמַעֲיָנֵי הֶעָנָן לַשָּׂדֶה וּמַעֲיָנֵי הַשָּׂדֶה לַדָּגָה שֶׁשָּׁטָה בּוֹ בְּדִמְיוֹנוּ
בֵּינוֹת לָעֲשָׂבִים, וּבַכְּרָמִים עֲנָבִים הוֹפְכִים לְצַמּוּקִים, אֲחֵרִים לְיַיִן, וְלֹא כָּל הַמָּתוֹק
נִגּוּעַ רִמַּת דְּאָגָה, וּמִי שֶׁמְּבַקֵּשׁ מַבּוּל אֵינוֹ מִתְכַּוֵּן לִכְלָיָה אֶלָּא רַק לְגֶשֶׁם חָזָק
וְקוֹלֵחַ, וּפַרְנְסֵי הַצִּבּוּר חוֹזְרִים מִן הַדֶּרֶךְ וְכוֹנְסִים לָהֶם מִשְׁפָּחָה, וְהַנְּדִיבוּת מִתְגַּלָּה
כִּסְגֻלָּה חֲרִישִׁית וְלֹא כְּמַעֲשֵׂה רַאֲוָה, וְהַטָּעֻיּוֹת מוּסָרוֹת מִלֵּב הַדְּבָרִים, וְחִלּוּף
הַחֲמָרִים הוֹגֵן, וּרְשׁוּת הָרַבִּים מְלֵאָה בִּרְשׁוּת וּרְשׁוּת הַיָּחִיד מְלֵאָה,

and the fruits have set a tenth aside and do not miss the
missing part, but are lighter, sweetness is intensified,
every branch that crossbreeds accedes to him with whom
it was crossbred, and the bulbs open themselves to the
outside, and the bees imagine the honey, and the trees
get themselves a new king according to the vigor of the
blooming, and the asphalt conquers the earth and liberates
the best of her on the side of the road,

and Tamar and Amnon have moved into a pansy, where
they are making cakes out of the colors, and the dust is
withdrawing before the pollination, and every drizzle is
the chance of a rainbow, and the green that is in the bushes
almost overwhelms the leaves, and in the old people's lawn
that surrounds you the water sprinklers of winter open,
and, indeed, there is suddenly a good southern wind,

only that she doesn't answer when you ask, sparing you the
nothingness, and her wrinkles multiply at once as if the
little girl inside her were shrinking her into herself, and
your words glide on the slope of her nose when you lean
on your cane, looking at her, looking at the blossoming,
looking at the asphalt (we could have lived so well, you say)
remembering the earth.

וְהַפֵּרוֹת מַפְרִישִׁים מַעֲשֵׂר וְלֹא מִתְגַּעְגְּעִים אֶל הַחֵלֶק הֶחָסֵר אֶלָּא קֵלִים יוֹתֵר
וּמְרֻכָּזֵי מְתִיקָה, וְכָל עָנָף שֶׁהֶכְלִיאוּ אוֹתוֹ מִתְרַצֶּה לְמִי שֶׁאֵתוֹ נִכְלָא, וְהַפְּקָעוֹת
מוֹשִׁיטוֹת עַצְמָן הַחוּצָה, וְהַדְּבוֹרִים מְדַמְיְנוֹת אֶת הַדְּבַשׁ, וְהָעֵצִים מַחֲלִיפִים לָהֶם
מֶלֶךְ לְפִי כֹּחַ הַפְּרִיחָה, וְהָאַסְפַלְט כּוֹבֵשׁ אֶת הָאֲדָמָה וּמְשַׁחְרֵר בְּצַד הַדֶּרֶךְ רַק אֶת
מֵיטָבָהּ,

וְהָאַמְנוֹן וְהַתָּמָר מְלַבְּבִים יַחַד לְבִיבוֹת שֶׁל צֶבַע, וְהָאָבָק נָסוֹג בִּפְנֵי הַהַאֲבָקָה, וְכָל
טִפָּטוּף הוּא סְכוּי לְקֶשֶׁת, וְהַיָּרֹק שֶׁבַּשִּׂיחִים כִּמְעַט מַכְרִיעַ אֶת הָעֲלָוָה, וּבַדֶּשֶׁא
הַזְּקֵנִים שֶׁסְּבִיבְכֶם נִפְתָּחוֹת מַמְטֵרוֹת הַחֹרֶף, וּבֶאֱמֶת יֵשׁ פִּתְאֹם רוּחַ דְּרוֹמִית
טוֹבָה,

רַק שֶׁהִיא לֹא עוֹנָה לְךָ כְּשֶׁאַתָּה שׁוֹאֵל, חוֹסֶכֶת מִמְּךָ אֶת הָאַיִן. קְמָטֶיהָ מִתְרַבִּים
בְּאַחַת, כְּמוֹ הָיְתָה הַיַּלְדָּה הַקְּטַנָּה בְּתוֹכָהּ מְכֻוֶּצֶת אוֹתָהּ אֵלֶיהָ. דְּבָרֶיךָ מַחֲלִיקִים
בְּמוֹרָד אַפָּהּ כְּשֶׁאַתָּה נִשְׁעָן עַל מַקֵּל הַהֲלִיכָה וּמַבִּיט בָּהּ, מַבִּיט בִּפְרִיחָה, מַבִּיט
בָּאַסְפַלְט (יָכֹלְנוּ לִחְיוֹת טוֹב כָּל כָּךְ, אַתָּה אוֹמֵר) זוֹכֵר אֶת הָאֲדָמָה.

SOON IT WILL BE DARK

Soon it will be dark.
The bicycles will carry the children up to the gate.
Their rapid arrival will burst into the house like boiling
    water.

Miles from here you will set a pot on the burner,
you will listen to the bubbling as if it were a sign of life.

The children will ask me to listen to how far they have
    been on their ride:
to the municipal road, even further,
to the intersection that keeps branching and branching
    and to the gas station and even further,
to old age, to the straight road,
the side street, the surprise one.
Excited, they will speak.
They have never gone so far.
Their shoes will testify with their dust.

At that same hour, you will be leaning on the balcony,
in the deserted path to your house the wind will blow,
a whistle will pass through the gap that divides
the branch from the leaf
and the leaf from the fruit,

a faint whistle,
almost a silence,
the voice of every thing,
and the voice of the distance between them
that holds everything in its place.

עוד מעט יחשיך

עוֹד מְעַט יַחְשִׁיךְ.
הָאוֹפַנַּיִם יִשְׂאוּ אֶת הַיְלָדִים עַד הַשַּׁעַר.
בּוֹאָם הַמָּהִיר יִכָּנֵס לְתוֹךְ הַבַּיִת כְּמוֹ מַיִם רוֹתְחִים.

אִישׁ לֹא יִטְרַח אָז עַל אֲרוּחָתֵךְ.
קִילוֹמֶטְרִים מִכָּאן תִּשְׁפֹּת אֶת הַסִּיר עַל הָאֵשׁ,
תַּאֲזִין לַבִּעְבּוּעַ כְּמוֹ לְאוֹת חַיִּים.

הַיְלָדִים יְבַקְשׁוּ שֶׁאַקְשִׁיב עַד כַּמָּה הִרְחִיקוּ בִּרְכִיבָתָם.
עַד לַכְּבִישׁ הָעִירוֹנִי וְהָלְאָה מִשָּׁם
אֶל הַמֶּחְלָפִים הַמִּסְתַּעֲפִים וּמִסְתַּעֲפִים וְעַד לְתַחֲנַת הַדֶּלֶק וְאַחֲרֶיהָ
עַד הַזִּקְנָה, עַד הַכְּבִישׁ הַיָּשָׁר, הַצְּדָדִי, הַמַּפְתִּיעַ.
הֵם יְדַבְּרוּ נִרְגָּשִׁים. מֵעוֹלָם לֹא הִגִּיעוּ רָחוֹק כָּל כָּךְ.
נַעֲלֵיהֶם יָעִידוּ עֲלֵיהֶם בְּאָבָק.
שָׁנִים רַבּוֹת יִצְטַבְּרוּ בְּבַת אַחַת עַל מִשְׁטַח הָעוֹר הַמָּתוּחַ.

בְּאוֹתָהּ שָׁעָה תִּשָּׁעֵן אַתָּה עַל הַמִּרְפֶּסֶת.
בִּשְׁבִיל הָרֵיק הַמּוֹבִיל אֶל בֵּיתְךָ תָּשֵׁב רוּחַ.
שְׁרִיקָה תַּעֲבֹר בָּרוּחַ הַמַּפְרִיד
בֵּין הֶעָנָף לֶעָלֶה
וּבֵין הֶעָלֶה לַפְּרִי.

שְׁרִיקָה דַּקָּה,
כִּמְעַט שְׁתִיקָה.
קוֹל הַדְּבָרִים,
וְקוֹל הַמֶּרְחָק בֵּינֵיהֶם
הַמַּחְזִיק כָּל דָּבָר בִּמְקוֹמוֹ.

FROM ETROG

*

A small body is placed on the bed
straight as a hyphen
between you-me.

**

And soon children hard as diamonds will circle you like a
    crown,
and soon you will straighten like the shaft of a feather,
and soon your first steps will accelerate into a run,
and soon you will be compelled to play hide-and-seek
with whomever tags you,

and the honey of love, which preserves you,
repels all touch that is not ready to stick, and soon
what will it help.

***

And I now say yes to the epidural, and yes to the aspirin,
and yes to the fallow years of *shmita*, to the talent wasted
on washing bottles and making the bed, yes to the belly
that hardens like a tree, and yes to the slingshot, the
constant balls of worry the hand releases, yes and yes, just
to see you sleep as if nothing changes around us when
you are.

****

Cotton wool in pillow and cotton wool in blanket,
cotton wool in teddy bear and cotton wool in doll,
I lay it all around you and wait
so that the world surrounding you will treat you like an
    etrog.

מתוך: אתרוג

*

גּוּף קָטָן מֻנָּח בַּמִּטָּה,
יָשָׁר כְּמוֹ הַמַּקָּף
בֵּין אֲנִי־אַתָּה.

**

וְעוֹד מְעַט יְלָדִים קָשִׁים כְּיַהֲלוֹם יַקִּיפוּ אוֹתְךָ כְּכֶתֶר,
וְעוֹד מְעַט תִּזְדַּקֵּף כְּמוֹ עוֹרֵק נוֹצָה,
וְעוֹד מְעַט צְעָדֶיךָ הָרִאשׁוֹנִים יָאִיצוּ לִמְרוּצָה,
וְעוֹד מְעַט כְּבָר תִּכְרַח לְשַׂחֵק מַחֲבוֹאִים
עִם מִי שֶׁמְּשַׂחֵק אִתְּךָ תּוֹפֶסֶת,

וְהַדְּבַשׁ שֶׁל הָאַהֲבָה הַמְשַׁמֵּר אוֹתְךָ
מֵנִיס כָּל מַגָּע שֶׁאֵינֶנּוּ מוּכָן לִדְבֹּק, עוֹד מְעַט
מַה יוֹעִיל.

***

אֲנִי אוֹמֶרֶת עַכְשָׁו כֵּן לָאֶפִּידוּרָל, וְכֵן לָאָקָמוֹל, וְכֵן לְשָׁנוֹת הַשֶּׁמְטָּה
שֶׁל הַכִּשָּׁרוֹן הַמְבֻזְבָּז עַל שְׁטִיפַת בַּקְבּוּקִים וְהִדּוּר הַמִּטָּה.
כֵּן לַקוֹל הַחוֹזֵר וּמִתְקַשֵּׁחַ וְעוֹדֵף,
וְכֵן לַבֶּטֶן הַמִּתְעַצָּה,
וְכֵן לְמִקְלַעַת הַיָּד הַמְשַׁחְרֶרֶת לְלֹא הֶרֶף כַּדּוּרֵי דְּאָגָה,
כֵּן וְכֵן,
רַק כְּדֵי לִרְאוֹת אוֹתְךָ יָשֵׁן,
כְּאִלּוּ כְּלוּם לֹא מִשְׁתַּנֶּה סָבִיב בְּעֵת שֶׁאַתָּה.

****

צֶמֶר גֶּפֶן בַּכָּרִית וְצֶמֶר גֶּפֶן בַּשְּׂמִיכָה,
צֶמֶר גֶּפֶן בַּדַּבּוֹן, וְצֶמֶר גֶּפֶן בַּבֻּבָּה,
אֲנִי מַנִּיחָה הַכֹּל סְבִיבְךָ וּמְחַכָּה,
שֶׁיַּעֲשֶׂה בְּךָ הָעוֹלָם כְּאֶתְרוֹג.

HEIR TO THE CURFEW

1.

Your body spills onto the bed. Good days. And only your hair, which is growing longer, stops me from being happy. This week you learned to walk. Soon you will be able to climb Mount Moriah, your brother Ishmael at your side, and which of you will continue to the ascent, now that there is no one but you to offer a ram in your place. My son, how is it that I do not extricate you, that I let time pass, your hair lengthen, bound in my hand while you sleep. Blindly groping, you find the nipple, and I offer you milk, anoint you with obligatory libations.

2.

And what has possession to do with your hair, which will be cut, no more ponytails, no more hands caressing the ponytails, cut short, like the time from here to the army, and to the curled-up cord of the telephone, busy at all hours, which, like girl-curls, our hands caress.

3.

Do not drink, my heir to the curfew, from the waters of conflict, the waters of Meribah. They bloat my stomach, and that of another woman whose son was killed in the shelling. She asked them to save her son—her second son—who was injured, but the concrete, but the solider (camp refugees equal refugee camps, heaps of what we will become if we do not stand strong) but the flow of the blood that stopped only in her eyes, which slowly went cold with the boy.

יורש העוצר

.1

גּוּפְךָ נִגָּר עַל הַמִּטָּה. יָמִים טוֹבִים. וְרַק שְׂעָרְךָ הַמִּתְאָרֵךְ עוֹצֵר מִבַּעֲדִי לִשְׂמֹחַ. הַשָּׁבוּעַ לָמַדְתָּ לָלֶכֶת. עוֹד מְעַט כְּבָר תּוּכַל לַעֲלוֹת בְּהַר הַמּוֹרִיָּה, אָחִיךָ יִשְׁמָעֵאל לְצִדְּךָ. וּמִי מִכֶּם יוֹסִיף וְיַעֲלֶה עַכְשָׁו כְּשֶׁאֵין אִישׁ זוּלַתְכֶם, לְהַצִּיעַ תַּחְתְּכֶם אֶת הָאַיִל. בְּנִי שֶׁלִּי, אֵיךְ אֵינֶנִּי מְמַלֶּטֶת אוֹתְךָ, נוֹתֶנֶת לַזְּמַן לַעֲבֹר, לַשַּׂעַר לְהִתְאָרֵךְ, לַיָּד שֶׁלְּךָ לְהִכָּרֵךְ עַל יָדִי מִתּוֹךְ שְׁנָתְךָ. מְגַשֵּׁשׁ עִוֵּר אַחֲרֵי הַפִּטְמָה אֲנִי מַצִּיעָה לְךָ חָלָב, מַזָּה עָלֶיךָ נִסְכֵּי חוֹבָה.

.2

וּמַה לַחֲזָקָה וְלִשְׂעָרְךָ שֶׁיִּתְקַצֵּר לִבְלִי קוּקְיּוֹת, לִבְלִי יָדַיִם הַלּוֹטְפוֹת קוּקְיּוֹת, יִתְקַצֵּר כְּמוֹ הַזְּמַן מִכָּאן וְעַד הַצָּבָא, וְעַד תַּלְתַּלֵּי הַטֶּלֶפוֹן הַפָּתוּחַ בְּכָל הַשָּׁעוֹת, שֶׁכְּמוֹ תַּלְתַּלֵּי בָּנוֹת יְלַטְּפוּ אֲרָכִים בְּיָדִי.

.3

אַל תִּשְׁתֶּה, יוֹרֵשׁ הָעֶצֶר שֶׁלִּי, מִמֵּי הַמְּרִיבָה. הֵם צָבִים אֶת בִּטְנִי, אֶת בִּטְנָהּ שֶׁל אַחֶרֶת שֶׁבְּנָהּ נֶהֱרַג בַּהַפְצָצָה. הִיא בִּקְשָׁה שֶׁיַּצִּילוּ אֶת בְּנָהּ הַשֵּׁנִי שֶׁנִּפְצַע, אֲבָל הַבָּטוֹן, אֲבָל הַחַיָּל (פְּלִיטֵי מַחֲנוֹת שָׁוֶה מַחֲנוֹת פְּלִיטִים, עֲרֵמָה שֶׁל מַה נִּהְיֶה אִם לֹא נִהְיֶה חֲזָקִים), אֲבָל זְרִימַת הַדָּם שֶׁנֶּעֶצְרָה רַק בְּעֵינֶיהָ, שֶׁקָּפְאוּ לְאַט עִם הַיֶּלֶד.

4.

Do not take part, my heir to the curfew, in the shelling; do
not take your father's uniform still smelling of the laundry,
don't mistake them for things in which there is no danger,
soap-free detergent, intention-free violence. Their smell
was once the smell of an olive tree uprooted to make room
for the destruction, in which you will not have a hand.

5.

Do not take part, my heir to the curfew, even in what
your mother says, for she hesitates and does not breach
the border of her house. The walls are blinders, her hands
are blinders on her eyes, closed this morning behind the
newspaper when she saw there what she saw. Even in her,
do not take part, leave her be in her house, and leave her,
for her wisdom has gone mad, otherwise, how to explain
that she, occupied by your sweetness, is not rising up to do
anything.

אַל תִּקַּח, יוֹרֵשׁ הֶעָצֵר שֶׁלִּי, חֵלֶק בַּהֲגִנָּה, אַל תִּקַּח אֶת מַדֵּי אָבִיךְ הָרֵיחָנִיִּים מִכְּבִיסָה, אַל תִּטְעֶה לַזֵהוֹת בָּהֶם דָּבָר שֶׁאֵין בּוֹ סַכָּנָה, סַבּוֹן נָטוּל סַבּוֹן, אַלִּימוּת נְטוּלַת כַּוָּנָה. רֵיחָם שֶׁהָיָה פַּעַם רֵיחַ זַיִת נֶעֱקָר כְּדֵי לְפַנּוֹת מָקוֹם לַדְּרִיסָה, שֶׁלֹּא תְּהֵא לְךָ בָּהּ רֶגֶל.

אַל תִּקַּח יוֹרֵשׁ הֶעָצֵר שֶׁלִּי חֵלֶק אֲפִלּוּ בְּקוֹלָהּ שֶׁל אִמְּךָ, שֶׁהִיא מְהַסֶּסֶת וְאֵינָהּ פּוֹרֶצֶת אֶת גְּבוּל בֵּיתָהּ. הַקִּירוֹת סָכִים עָלֶיהָ, סָכִים עַל יָדֶיהָ הַסָּכוֹת עַל עֵינֶיהָ שֶׁנֶּעֶצְמוּ הַבֹּקֶר אֶל מוּל הֶעָתוֹן כְּשֶׁרָאֲתָה מַה שֶׁרָאֲתָה. אֲפִלּוּ בָּהּ אַל תִּקַּח חֵלֶק, הַשְׁאֵר אוֹתָהּ בְּבֵיתָהּ וַעֲזֹב אוֹתָהּ שֶׁנִּטְרְפָה בִּינָתָהּ, אַחֶרֶת כֵּיצַד לְהַסְבִּיר שֶׁהִיא כְּבוּשַׁת מְתִיקוּתְךָ, אֵינָהּ קָמָה לַעֲשׂוֹת דָּבָר.

When you are with me in the room I forget more than I remember

Island

כְּשֶׁאַתָּה אִתִּי בַּחֶדֶר אֲנִי יוֹתֵר שׁוֹכַחַת מְזֹכֶרֶת

אִי

The woman from the lock company calls to ask if I'd be interested in a steel door for the protection of *those who dwell in the house*. Really, I am so careful all the time not to forget to fill out a single form or anything. The income tax assessor smiles at me. One part of him is already melting coins down into metal. And beyond him is a wall, and beyond the wall, a wall, and beyond that, how does it happen that I am relaxing in a chair, listening to technical specifications, floating inside a hiss, the taxes of my hands have been thrown into the sea, and I am reading poetry, hugging the baby and evading his future, sleep, sleep, for *if a man comes to kill you, rise early* . . . I cover the door with blankets of locks (and during the *ne'ila*, the closing of heaven's gates, of whom should I ask forgiveness), behold, the rising water.

הָאִשָּׁה מֵחֲבֶרֶת הַבְּרִיחַ מִתְקַשֶּׁרֶת לִשְׁאֹל אִם אֶרְצֶה דֶּלֶת פְּלָדָה, מְגִנָּה
עַל יוֹשְׁבֵי הַבַּיִת. בֶּאֱמֶת, אֲנִי כָּל כָּךְ זְהִירָה כָּל הָעֵת לֹא לִשְׁכּׁחַ טִפֶּס
אוֹ מָה. פְּקִיד הַשּׁוּמָה מְחַיֵּךְ אֵלַי, קְצֵהוּ הָאַחֵר כְּבָר מַתִּיךְ מַטְבְּעוֹת
לְמַתֶּכֶת. וּמֵעֵבֶר לוֹ יֵשׁ חוֹמָה וּמֵעֵבֶר לַחוֹמָה, חוֹמָה, וּמֵעֵבֶר לָהּ מַה לִּי
שֶׁאֲנִי מִתְרַוַּחַת בְּתוֹךְ כְּסָא מַקְשִׁיבָה לַמְּפָרֵט הַטְּכְנִי, נָעָה בְּתוֹךְ אֻוְשָׁה,
מַסֵּי יָדַי מַטְבִּיעִים בַּיָּם וַאֲנִי קוֹרֵאת שִׁירָה, מְחַבֶּקֶת אֶת הַתִּינוֹק
וּמִשְׁתַּמֶּטֶת מֵעֲתִידוֹ, שֵׁן, שֵׁן, מִי שֶׁיָּקוּם לְהָרְגוֹ, מְכַסָּה אֶת הַדֶּלֶת בִּשְׂמִיכַת
מַנְעוּלִים (וּבִשְׁעַת נְעִילָה מִמִּי אֲבַקֵּשׁ מְחִילָה) הִנֵּה הַמַּיִם עוֹלִים.

I am Isaac in reverse.
First I recognize your voice and only afterward I become
    blind,
once as a mistake, once as a blessing.

Moving backward from there I am Abraham.
I do not care who will save us more
the god or the ram,
as long as we ascend together.

Moving backward from there, your body curves
in my round stomach like an apple.
And the tree that is standing and the snake that is
    reclining
are hinges that cannot measure us
who sneak into the interior garden.

Maybe love will stop here.
Another step back, the formlessness and void,
another step forward,
the formlessness and void to come.

The future and its collaborator, the present

אֲנִי יִצְחָק הֶהָפוּךְ.
קֹדֶם מַכִּירָה אֶת קוֹלְךָ וְרַק אַחַר כָּךְ מִתְעוֹרֶרֶת.
פַּעַם לְטָעוּת, פַּעַם לִבְרָכָה.

אָחוֹרָה מִשָּׁם אֲנִי אַבְרָהָם.
לֹא אִכְפַּת לִי מִי יַצִּיל אוֹתָנוּ יוֹתֵר
הָאֵל אוֹ הָאַיִל,
כָּל עוֹד נַעֲלֶה יַחְדָּו.

אָחוֹרָה מִשָּׁם גּוּפְךָ מִתְקַמֵּר
בְּבִטְנִי הָעֲגֻלָּה כְּתַפּוּחַ.
וְהָעֵץ הָעוֹמֵד וְהַנָּחָשׁ הַשׁוֹכֵב
הֵם צִירִים שֶׁלֹּא יוּכְלוּ לִמְדֹּד אוֹתָנוּ
שֶׁחוֹמְקִים לַגָּן הַפְּנִימִי.

אוּלַי תַּעֲצֹר פֹּה הָאַהֲבָה.
עוֹד צַעַד אָחוֹרָה הַתֹּהוּ וָבֹהוּ,
עוֹד צַעַד קָדִימָה
הַתֹּהוּ וָבֹהוּ הַבָּא.

Boy   Mother

                          yes   yes   yes

                   Morse code signaling distress

a
r
e

t
r
a
v
e
l
i
n
g

u
p

t
o

u
s

כֵּן כֵּן כֵּן

מוֹרְס קָצָר מְבַקֵּשׁ הַצָּלָה

Toward morning I found a blind cat at the threshold of the house. Thin pus from I can't see where. For a long time I fluttered around the living room looking for the opening to the bedroom, but repose was for someone else, for the one who hadn't opened the door. I had a telephone, cotton wool, and a cat doctor on duty,

I walked up to him on the gravel path, a dead-end street in my hands.

What made the blind cat hang on to me like this as I was walking, what made him not hear my feet, which are retreating back into the walking, what caused him to lick my hand, which is disgusted with the contact, pus, pus, what made me suddenly imagine my son in uniform at such an hour of the morning, he doesn't know when the evil will open on him, more than the evil that he has already done (camp refugees equal refugee camps, heaps of what we will become if we don't stand strong), what caused the silent sobbings and the fear of the dark (*soldiers soldiers fire our village devoured*) and the fear of the telephone cord, which twists even more in my hand when I won't ask whom has he hit, and this blind cat, what is to be done, I won't flee this place, I will remain in the waiting room, waiting for him to emerge wrapped in a towel, and here he comes now, the examination over (equal sign getting narrower and narrower, closing in on our house like a two-sided monument, like a strait) and it's really recommended to put the cat to sleep, a common, inexpensive procedure, after which there will be silence, so he won't suffer anymore, so he'll really close his eyes.

לִפְנוֹת בֹּקֶר מָצָאתִי חָתוּל עִוֵּר עַל סַף הַבַּיִת. מְגֻלָּה דַּקָּה שֶׁל אֵינֶנִּי רוֹאָה. שָׁעָה אֲרֻכָּה חַגְתִּי בַּסָּלוֹן מְחַפֶּשֶׂת פֶּתַח אֶל חֲדַר הַשֵּׁנָה, אֲבָל הַמְּנוּחָה הָיְתָה לָאַחַר שֶׁלֹּא פָּתַח אֶת הַדֶּלֶת. לִי הָיָה טֶלֶפוֹן, צֶמֶר גֶּפֶן, רוֹפֵא חֲתוּלִים תּוֹרָן,

הָלַכְתִּי אֵלָיו בִּשְׁבִיל הַכְּרְכָּר וּרְחוֹב לְלֹא מוֹצָא בְּיָדִי.

מַה גָּרַם לֶחָתוּל הָעִוֵּר לְהֵאָחֵז בִּי כָּכָה כְּשֶׁהָלַכְתִּי, מַה גָּרַם לוֹ לֹא לִשְׁמֹעַ אֶת רַגְלֵי הַנְּסוֹגוֹת אָחוֹר בְּתוֹךְ הֲלִיכָה, מַה גָּרַם לוֹ לְלַקֵּק אֶת יָדִי הַנִּגְעֶלֶת מִכָּל מַגָּע, מְגֻלָּה מְגֻלָּה, מַה גָּרַם לִי לְדַמְיֵן פִּתְאֹם אֶת בְּנֵי בְּמַדִּים בִּשְׁעַת בֹּקֶר כָּזוֹ, לֹא יוֹדֵעַ מָתַי תִּפָּתַח עָלָיו הָרָעָה יוֹתֵר מִן הָרָעָה שֶׁכְּבָר עָשָׂה (פְּלִיטֵי מַחֲנוֹת שָׁוֶה מַחֲנוֹת פְּלִיטִים, עֲרֵמָה שֶׁל מַה נִּהְיֶה אִם לֹא נִהְיֶה חֲזָקִים), מַה גָּרַם לְיַלְלוֹת הַשְּׁקֵטוֹת וְלַפַּחַד מִן הַחֲשֵׁכָה (חַיָּלִים חַיָּלִים שְׂרֵפָה עֲיָרָתֵנוּ טָרֹף טָרְפָה) וּלְחוּט הַטֶּלֶפוֹן שֶׁיִּתְפַּתֵּל עוֹד בְּיָדִי כְּשֶׁלֹּא אֶשְׁאַל בְּמִי פָּגַע, וְהֶחָתוּל הָעִוֵּר הַזֶּה, מָה אֲנִי עוֹשָׂה, לֹא אֶבְרַח מִפֹּה, אֶשָּׁאֵר בַּחֲדַר הַהַמְתָּנָה לְחַכּוֹת לוֹ עָטוּף בְּמַגֶּבֶת, וְהִנֵּה הוּא כְּבָר יוֹצֵא, הַסְתָּיְמָה הַבְּדִיקָה (סִימָן הַשָּׁוֶה הוֹלֵךְ וְצַר, סוֹגֵר עַל בֵּיתִי כְּאַנְדַּרְטָה לִשְׁנֵי צְדָדִים, כְּמֶצֶר), וּמַמְלִיץ בֶּאֱמֶת לְהַרְדִּים, פְּעֻלָּה זוֹלָה, אַחֲרֶיהָ שְׁתִיקָה, שֶׁלֹּא יִסְבֹּל יוֹתֵר, שֶׁבֶּאֱמֶת יַעֲצֹם עֵינַיִם.

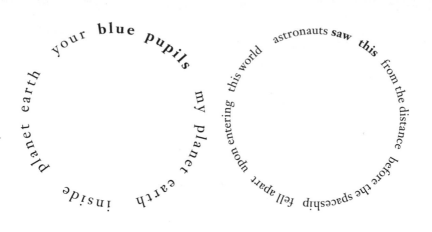

The air is the silence it is waiting

הָאֲוִיר הוּא הַשֶּׁקֶט וְהוּא מְחַכֶּה.

Boy, there is peat from under the swamp that they dried out before we got here; it is about to become a swamp of fire. Now just get out,[1] the dot on the ground, which you see from your window, is me shrinking into myself to make room in the world for your travels.

Or even better, don't go out[2] and we will upholster the walls with more books. Not to save us, but to augment our weight, to sink together, comforted in the depths. We will remain embraced. The word *mother* will be fixed around you, its beginning is from the beginning, like a strip of internal time, holiday after holiday.

---

1. Don't cry with Esau when he discovered that the hand of his father didn't really recognize him, didn't stroke his hair.

Don't cry with Jacob when Rachel was revealed to him, and all the years were spread before him, replacing her again and again with another weary woman.

Don't even cry with Joseph when, before his lost family, he realized how deep the pit was and to what extent he was, indeed, devoured, just as they had said, torn and devoured with no way back.

2. Don't cry, laugh, with that worthy thing that revives itself: Rachel's Jacob, the brothers' Joseph, even Esau, who kisses his father, to be loving if not beloved. Turn to God, my son, turn to some god and you will be redeemed within all this "our ancestors," and this "our children," and all the mediations, which again and again deceive.

יֶלֶד, תַּחַת הַבִּצָּה שֶׁיִּבְּשׁוּ לְפָנֵינוּ עוֹמֶדֶת אַדְמַת כָּבוּל לִהְיוֹת לְבִצָּה שֶׁל אֵשׁ. לֹא הִצִּיל אוֹתִי רְצוֹנוֹ הַשּׁוֹאֵב שֶׁל אָבִי, וְלֹא יַצִּיל אוֹתְךָ רְצוֹנִי הַמְכַסֶּה. עַכְשָׁו רַק צֵא[1] הַנְּקֻדָּה שֶׁתִּרְאֶה מֵחַלּוֹנְךָ עַל הַקַּרְקַע זוֹ אֲנִי הַמְכֻוֶּצֶת עַצְמִי לְהוֹתִיר אֶת כָּל הָעוֹלָם לְמַסְעוֹתֶיךָ.

אוֹ מוּטָב, אַל תֵּצֵא[2] וּנְרַפֵּד אֶת הַקִּירוֹת בְּעוֹד סְפָרִים. לֹא לְהַצִּיל כִּי אִם לְהַגְדִּיל אֶת מִשְׁקָלֵנוּ, לִשְׁקֹעַ יַחַד, מְנֻחָמִים מִן הַמַּעֲמַקִּים. נִשָּׁאֵר חֲבוּקִים. הַמִּלָּה אִמָּא תִּתְפַּס סְבִיבְךָ, רֹאשָׁהּ בִּתְחִלָּתָהּ, כְּמוֹ רְצוּעָה שֶׁל זְמַן פְּנִימִי, חַג וְחַג.

---

1. אל תבכה עם עשׂו כשגילה שיד אביו לא הכירה אותו באמת, לא ליטפה את שׂערו. אל תבכה עם יעקב כשנגלתה לו רחל, וכל השנים נפרשׂו לפניו, מחליפות אותה שוב ושוב באישה לאה אחרת.
אל תבכה אפילו עם יוסף כשהבין מול משפחתו האבודה עד כמה עמוק הבור, וכמה באמת טורף כמו שאמרו, טורף ללא חזור.

2. אל תבכה, צְחַק, ממה שראוי להתחיות ממנו: יעקב של רחל, יוסף של אחיו, אפילו עשׂו שנושק לאביו, להיות אוהב אם לא נאהב. מְצָא לך אל, בני. מְצָא אל מי ותיגאל. בתוך כל האבותינו הזה והילדינו הזה, והתווך, ששוב ושוב מכזיב.

And if fire comes to punish us,
it will come as a new deluge,
to counterbalance what our forefathers got in the water.[3]

To restore the world to itself, believing again in the field.

---

3. The air is the silence and it is waiting.

וְאִם אֵשׁ תָּבוֹא לְהַעֲנִישֵׁנוּ,
תָּבוֹא כְּמַבּוּל חָדָשׁ,
לְאַזֵּן אֶת מַה שֶׁקִּבְּלוּ אֲבוֹתֵינוּ בְּמַיִם.[3]

לְהָשִׁיב אֶת הָעוֹלָם אֶל עַצְמוֹ, מַאֲמִין בַּשֵּׁנִית בַּשָּׂדֶה.

---

3. הָאֲוִיר הוּא הַשֶּׁקֶט וְהוּא מְחַכֶּה.

BEGGAR

You promised me, you say.
So I promised, I say.
And the words create a bowl,
and they knock against it like a beggar.

You promised me, you say.
So I promised, I say.
And the words create a bowl,
and they knock against it like a beggar.

You promised me, you say.
So I promised, I say.
And the words create a bowl,
and they knock against it like a beggar.

קבצן

הִבְטַחְתָּ לִי, אַתָּה אוֹמֵר.
אָז הִבְטַחְתִּי, אֲנִי אוֹמֶרֶת.
וְהַמִּלִּים בּוֹרְאוֹת קְעָרָה
וְנוֹקְשׁוֹת עָלֶיהָ כְּמוֹ קַבְצָן.

הִבְטַחְתָּ לִי, אַתָּה אוֹמֵר.
אָז הִבְטַחְתִּי, אֲנִי אוֹמֶרֶת.
וְהַמִּלִּים בּוֹרְאוֹת קְעָרָה
וְנוֹקְשׁוֹת עָלֶיהָ כְּמוֹ קַבְּצָן.

הִבְטַחְתָּ לִי, אַתָּה אוֹמֵר.
אָז הִבְטַחְתִּי, אֲנִי אוֹמֶרֶת.
וְהַמִּלִּים בּוֹרְאוֹת קְעָרָה
וְנוֹקְשׁוֹת עָלֶיהָ כְּמוֹ קַבְּצָן.

THE LOVE, YONATAN

*When you lift yourself to each other's lips—sip to sip—oh how
strangely each drinker slips away from his plot.*
RILKE, *DUINO ELEGIES*

1.

Wherefore Yonatan fell in love with David:
for the shape of his moving lips in the pronunciation of
    his name,
for their closing after speaking
as if turning from a bow into an arrow
flying far into the distance to mark
the portion that is far from him.

2.

Bottle of soy substituting for milk,
bottle of squeezed juice faking the fruit,
bottle of mineral water we suddenly started to drink
fearing the lead from the tap.
Waiting for recycling, they stand beside the cupboard
measuring our time in liters.
Where is the fullness that used to be in them,
and now is in us?

3.

Oh Yonatan, Yehonatan, Yonatan,
where God comes out of his name
like the needle of a sewing machine,
basting it, the stitch of love, sewn
onto the clothing of the king.

הָאַהֲבָה, יוֹנָתָן

"הַעוֹד אַתֶּם אוֹהֲבִים? שָׁעָה שֶׁאַתֶּם מְרִימִים
זֶה אֶת זֶה אֶל פִּיכֶם וְנוֹגְעִים – שִׁקּוּי אֶל שִׁקּוּי:
מוּזָר אֵיךְ נִתַּק הַשּׁוֹתֶה בְּעוֹד הוּא עוֹשֶׂה מַעֲשֵׂהוּ."
רַיְינֶר מַרְיָה רִילְקֶה,
אֱלֶגְיוֹת דוּאִינוֹ
(תרגום: שמעון זנדבנק)

.1

עַל שׁוּם מָה הִתְאַהֵב יוֹנָתָן בְּדָוִד, עַל שׁוּם
צוּרַת שְׂפָתָיו הַנָּעוֹת עֵת בִּטֵּא אֶת שְׁמוֹ.
עַל שׁוּם סְגִירָתָן לְאַחַר דַּבְּרוֹ
כְּמוֹ הוֹפְכוֹת מִקֶּשֶׁת לְחֵץ,
וְעָפוֹת הַרְחֵק לְסַמֵּן לוֹ:
הַחֵצִי מִמֶּנּוּ וָהָלְאָה.

.2

בַּקְבּוּק מֵי הַסּוֹיָה הַמַּחֲלִיפִים אֶת הֶחָלָב,
בַּקְבּוּק הַמִּיץ הַסָּחוּט הַמְזַיֵּף אֶת הַפְּרִי,
בַּקְבּוּק הַמַּיִם הַמִּינֶרָלְיִים שֶׁהִתְחַלְנוּ לִשְׁתּוֹת פִּתְאֹם
מֵחֲשָׁשׁ לְעוֹפֶרֶת בַּבֶּרֶז.
מְחַכִּים לְמִחְזוּר הֵם עוֹמְדִים בְּצַד הָאָרוֹן
מוֹדְדִים אֶת זְמַנֵּנוּ בְּלִיטְרִים.
אֵיפֹה הַמְּלֵאוּת שֶׁהָיְתָה בָּהֶם
וְכָעֵת הִיא בָּנוּ?

.3

הוּ יוֹנָתָן, יְהוֹנָתָן, יוֹנָתָן
שֶׁהָאֵל בָּא יוֹצֵא מִשְּׁמוֹ
כְּמוֹ מַחֲטֵי מְכוֹנַת תְּפִירָה,
מַכְלִיב אוֹתוֹ תַּךְ אַהֲבָה הַתָּפוּר
עַל בִּגְדֵי הַמֶּלֶךְ

4.

Sometimes at night
we sit chatting,
the children sleeping,
the housework not demanding
more than a ten percent offering.

I look at you and think,
I, too, fell in love with you once
only for that you spoke.

That portion is far from us.

5.

Oh Yonatan, Yehonatan,
out of pity you die,
so you wouldn't see how David ages,
writing Uriah the note.
His heart was given to the blankness with which
     everything had been shined:
his absence set you running to search the field,
the bother, the exhaustion, and your bow,
which was placed on the mountain beside your father's bow,
finally completing the cycle.

Oh Yonatan, Yehonatan, Yonatan,
your love pours red into his hair.
But what clung to him
when he grew old in the clothes of the king,
and all the blazing that was in you
seemed to him a pyre.

לִפְעָמִים, בַּלֵּילוֹת,
אֲנַחְנוּ מְסֻבִּים לְשׁוֹחֵחַ.
הַיְלָדִים כְּבָר יְשֵׁנִים,
מְלֶאכֶת הַבַּיִת אֵינָהּ תּוֹבַעַת
מִנְחָה גְּדוֹלָה מִמַּעֲשֵׂר.

עֵינֶיךָ הָעִרְנִיּוֹת שֶׁל הַבֹּקֶר
מִתְחַלְּפוֹת בְּעֵינֶיךָ הַנִּסְגָּרוֹת לְאַט.
אֲנִי מַבִּיטָה בְּךָ וְחוֹשֶׁבֶת:
גַּם אֲנִי הִתְאַהַבְתִּי בְּךָ פַּעַם
רַק כֵּיוָן שֶׁדִּבַּרְתָּ.

הַחֵצִי מֵאִתָּנוּ וָהָלְאָה.

.5

הוּ יוֹנָתָן יְהוֹנָתָן
מְרַחֲמִים אַתָּה מֵת.
שֶׁלֹּא תִּרְאֶה אֵיךְ דָּוִד מִזְדַּקֵּן,
כּוֹתֵב לְאוּרִיָּה אֶת הַפֶּתֶק.
לִבּוֹ נָתוּן לַסֶּרֶק שֶׁבּוֹ מוּרָק הַכֹּל:
הֶעָדְרוֹ שֶׁהֶרַיִץ אוֹתְךָ לְחַפֵּשׂ בַּשָּׂדֶה,
הַסְּרֵחָה, הָעֲיֵפוּת, וְהַקֶּשֶׁת שֶׁלְּךָ
שֶׁהֻנְּחָה עַל הָהָר לְיַד קֶשֶׁת אָבִיךָ,
מַשְׁלִימָה סוֹף-סוֹף מַעְגָּל שָׁלֵם.

הוּ יוֹנָתָן יְהוֹנָתָן יוֹנָתָן
אַהֲבָתְךָ מָזְגָה בִּשְׂעָרוֹ אָדֹם.
אֲבָל מַה נֶּאֱחַז בּוֹ מִבְּלִי שֶׁיֵּצַן
כְּשֶׁזָּקֵן בְּבִגְדֵי הַמֶּלֶךְ,
וְכָל הַבְּעֵרָה שֶׁהָיְתָה בְּךָ
נִדְמְתָה לוֹ כְּמוֹקֵד.

6.

Years later in the desert they found
the bones of the king
long as drumsticks.
You recognized them
from the power of their touch,
cradled them in your hands,
whispered things to them,
how in the beginning he played for Saul,
afterward, he played on you,
his hands in the baskets of foreskins,
pinching heart shapes,
his head is pulled back,
he is not one of the vacuous ones,
his hands played on the harp,
but his guts intended drums.

7.

Nor did we ascend to heaven in the blazing chariot of
    our love.
We were scattered into the house like rice and lentils.
The weight I gained, I gained to be closer to the ground,
to desire the gods less.
Even like this
I would take you again,
until I held your wrinkled hand,
folded like a shirt I wore.
Until I led you, exhausted,
swaddling you in a blanket,
until I knew myself in you
and whispered: even now.

6.

בַּמִּדְבָּר אַחֲרֵי שָׁנִים מָצְאוּ
אֶת עַצְמוֹת הַמֶּלֶךְ
אֲרֻכּוֹת כְּמוֹ מַקְלוֹת לְתֻפִּים.
עִרְסַלְתָּ אוֹתָן בְּיָדֶיךָ
לַחֲשֹׁתָ לָהֶן דְּבָרִים:
אֵיךְ תְּחִלָּה נִגֵּן לְשָׁאוּל,
אַחַר-כָּךְ נִגֵּן עָלֶיךָ,
יָדָיו בְּסַלֵּי הָעֲרֵלוֹת
לִצְבֹּט צוּרוֹת שֶׁל לֵב,
רֹאשׁוֹ מָשׁוּךְ אָחוֹר
אֵינֶנּוּ אַחַד הָרֵיקִים,
יָדָיו נִגְּנוּ עַל הַנֵּבֶל
אֲבָל תּוֹכוֹ הִתְכַּוֵּן תֻּפִּים.

7.

גַּם אֲנַחְנוּ לֹא עָלִינוּ הַשָּׁמַיְמָה בְּמֶרְכָּבָה בּוֹעֶרֶת מֵאַהֲבָתֵנוּ.
נִפְרַטְנוּ אֶל תּוֹךְ הַבַּיִת כְּמוֹ אֹרֶז וּכְמוֹ עֲדָשִׁים.
הַמִּשְׁקָל שֶׁהֶעֱלֵיתִי, הֶעֱלֵיתִי כְּדֵי לִקְרַב יוֹתֵר לַקַּרְקַע,
לִרְצוֹת פָּחוֹת לָאֵלִים.
אֲבָל אֶפְשָׁר גַּם כָּךְ אֲנִי אוֹמֶרֶת, גַּם כָּךְ
אֶקַּח אוֹתְךָ שׁוּב,
עַד שֶׁאֶזְכֶּה לְהַחֲזִיק בְּיָדְךָ הַמִּתְקַמֶּטֶת
כְּקִפּוּלֵי חַלְצָה שֶׁלָּבַשְׁתִּי.
עַד שֶׁאֶזְכֶּה לְהוֹלִיךְ אוֹתְךָ עָיֵף
וּלְחַתֵּל אוֹתְךָ בִּשְׂמִיכָה,
עַד שֶׁאֶזְכֶּה לְהַכִּיר בְּךָ אֶת פְּנֵי
וְלִלְחֹשׁ: עֲדַיִן.

8.

Oh Yonatan, Yehonatan, Yonatan,
the name embroidered on the blanket of the king,
but he is coming, departing from his wife,
to unravel you back.
The love, Yonatan, is constantly emptying,
but the body that remembers
is strong as a plastic bottle
that refuses to disintegrate.

9.

So we are also ready for the night,
the fingers spread to embrace
are like spears we have thrown,
but it is also possible to say
that they are like
strings of a harp.
When the wind approaches us
they play a tune,
and for a moment
we are holding the robe of the king
whom we have crowned.
For one moment, Yonatan, everything
seeks and finds.
For one moment, everything
is not borrowed, is not Shaul.

.8

הוֹ יוֹנָתָן יְהוֹנָתָן יוֹנָתָן
שֶׁנִּרְקַם עַל שְׂמִיכַת הַמֶּלֶךְ,
אֲבָל הוּא בָּא יוֹצֵא מֵאִשְׁתּוֹ
לִפְרֹם אוֹתְךָ בַּחֲזָרָה.
הָאַהֲבָה, יוֹנָתָן, מִתְרוֹקֶנֶת בְּלִי הֶרֶף,
אֲבָל הַגּוּף שֶׁזּוֹכֵר,
חָזָק כְּמוֹ בַּקְבּוּק שֶׁל פְּלַסְטִיק,
עֲקֵשׁ לְהִוָּתֵר.

.9

הִנֵּה גַּם אֲנַחְנוּ נְכוֹנִים לַלַּיְלָה,
וְהָאֶצְבָּעוֹת הַפְּרוּשׂוֹת לְחַבֵּק הֵן
כְּמוֹ חֲנִיתוֹת שֶׁהֻשְׁלַכְנוּ,
אֲבָל אֶפְשָׁר גַּם לוֹמַר אַחֶרֶת,
שֶׁהֵן כְּמוֹ
מֵיתָרִים שֶׁל נֵבֶל.
כְּשֶׁסְּעָרָה הָרוּחַ אֵלֵינוּ
הֵן מְנַגְּנוֹת מַנְגִּינָה
וּלְהֶרֶף,
אֲנַחְנוּ אוֹחֲזִים בִּגְלִימַת הַמֶּלֶךְ
שֶׁאֲנַחְנוּ הִמְלַכְנוּ.
לְרֶגַע אֶחָד, יוֹנָתָן, הַכֹּל מְחַפֵּשׂ וּמוֹצֵא.
לְרֶגַע אֶחָד,
לֹא הַכֹּל שָׁאוּל.

BIRD

And when we go out a bird will fly
over the cave,
and all the earth will shine with her light.

And we will know that you and I suffice for our world.
Look, years have ended without that bird,
and we are not missing a thing.

צִיפּוֹר

וּכְשֶׁנֵּצֵא תָּעוּף צִפּוֹר
מֵעַל הַמְּעָרָה,
כָּל הָאָרֶץ תַּבְרִיק מְאוֹרָה.

וְנֵדַע שֶׁדַּי לְעוֹלָמֵנוּ אֲנִי וְאַתָּה.
הִנֵּה תַּמּוּ שָׁנִים בִּלְעָדֶיהָ
וְלֹא נִגְרַע מֵאִתָּנוּ דָּבָר.

FROM
Cradle

I CALL TO TELL A FRIEND
THAT MY MOTHER IS DYING

I moved apartments three times in three years—it still
beats buying, in my opinion. Who knows how long this
   country will last.

The children, the work, there's never enough time,
I just called to hear your voice.

Awful things going on in the world.
How are you?

אני מתקשרת לספר לחבר שאמא שלי גוססת

שָׁלֹשׁ דִּירוֹת עָבַרְתִּי בְּשָׁלֹשׁ שָׁנִים, זֶה עֲדַיִן עָדִיף בְּעֵינַי
עַל פְּנֵי לִקְנוֹת. לֹא בָּרוּר כַּמָּה הַמְּדִינָה הַזֹּו תַּחְזִיק.

הַיְלָדִים, הָעֲבוֹדָה, אֵין מַסְפִּיק זְמַן, סְתָם,
הִתְקַשַּׁרְתִּי לִשְׁמֹעַ אוֹתְךָ.

דְּבָרִים נוֹרָאִים קוֹרִים בָּעוֹלָם.
מַה שְׁלוֹמְךָ?

REVERSE SATI

And when they lower her down to the pit only he sees
that she is on fire // not the public whispering not the
obsequious flattery // live fire as at Varanasi on the river //
anointed with the oil of her name he is drawing recklessly
near // in a moment he will hurl himself back into life
without her and he will have to live it with no police
intervention to save him, to stop the ceremony on charges
of unspeakable cruelty // just now the miracle of breathing
is shining from within him // every upright body seems
to him a wonder // how is it that // now joy is permeating
him // all his limbs are phantom pain and her beauty is a
real limb // everyone is watching if we don't save him //
from his fate, we'll save him from the anonymity of
fate // the roar of the bound is greater // than the roar of
the torched // what will become of all this // what could
come // what frightens the drowning is not the water but
the quiet // what frightens the sacrifice is not the pain but
the insult // but he who takes a fire to his bosom will not
be impoverished // for greater is the bush that burned
and was consumed than the bush that never burned // for
greater is the flesh to flesh than the from dust to dust // for
the main thing is the love // is // only the main thing is the
main thing // not the narrow bridge.

SATI PRATHA

וּכְשֶׁמּוֹרִידִים אוֹתָהּ אֶל הַבּוֹר רַק הוּא רוֹאֶה שֶׁהִיא עוֹלָה
בָּאֵשׁ // לֹא הַקָּהָל הַמְלַחֵשׁ, לֹא הַכִּסּוּי הַמִּתְרַפֵּס // אֵשׁ חַיָּה
כְּמוֹ בְּרָאנְסִי בַּנָּהָר // מָשׁוּחַ בְּשֶׁמֶן שְׁמָהּ הוּא מִתְקָרֵב וְלֹא
נִזְהָר // עוֹד רֶגַע יַשְׁלִיךְ עַצְמוֹ חֲזָרָה אֶל הַחַיִּים בִּלְעָדֶיהָ, וְיִהְיֶה
עָלָיו לִחְיוֹת בָּהֶם בְּלִי שֶׁאַף מִשְׁטָרָה תַּצִּיל אוֹתוֹ וְתַעֲצֹר אֶת
הַשֶּׁקֶט בְּאַשְׁמַת אַכְזָרִיּוּת נוֹרָאָה // אֵיךְ זֶה שֶׁדַּוְקָא עַכְשָׁו זוֹרֵחַ
מִתּוֹכוֹ הַנֵּס שֶׁל הַנְּשִׁימָה // כָּל גּוּף זָקוּף נִרְאֶה לוֹ פֶּלֶא // אֵיךְ
זֶה שֶׁדַּוְקָא // עַכְשָׁו מִתְרַחֶבֶת בּוֹ שִׂמְחָה // אֵיבָרָיו הֵם כְּאָב
הַפַּנְטוֹם וְיָפְיָהּ אֵיבָר אֱמֶת // הַכֹּל מַבְּיטִים, אִם לֹא לְהַצִּיל
אוֹתוֹ מִגּוֹרָלוֹ, לְהַצִּיל אוֹתוֹ מֵאַלְמוֹנִיּוּת הַגּוֹרָל // שַׁאֲגַת הַנֶּעֱקָד
חֲזָקָה // מִשַּׁאֲגַת הַמְּבֹעָר // מַה מִכָּל זֶה יַהֲפֹךְ, יוּכַל לַהֲפֹךְ
לְעָבָר // מַה שֶׁמַּפְחִיד אֶת הַטּוֹבֵעַ הוּא לֹא הַמַּיִם אֶלָּא הַשֶּׁקֶט //
מַה שֶׁמַּפְחִיד אֶת הָעוֹלֶה הוּא לֹא הַכְּאֵב אֶלָּא הָעִלָּבוֹן // אֲבָל
הוּא, אֲשֶׁר חָתָה יֵשׁ בְּקִרְבּוֹ, וְאֵיךְ יִתְרוֹשֵׁשׁ // דּוֹלֵק גֵּאֶה
וּמְפֹאָר // שֶׁגָּדוֹל הַסְּנֶה שֶׁבָּעַר וְאֻכַּל מִן הַסְּנֶה שֶׁלֹּא בָּעַר //
שֶׁגָּדוֹל בָּשָׂר לְבָשָׂר מֵעָפָר לְעָפָר // שֶׁרַק הָעִקָּר הוּא הָעִקָּר, לֹא
הַגֶּשֶׁר הַצַּר // רַק הָאַהֲבָה הִיא דָבָר.

YEARNING CRUMBS

Return, return, I am waiting in the kitchen. How did
you know to teach me that the flour is the Torah and
the kneading calms the yeast like the flocks before the
slaughter, that the general opens into the private with the
password of the hands, and that in the vanilla there is no
cheating.

When you were alive there were entire days I could not
think about you
and now there are entire days I can.

Without admitting it, everyone with a mother is a suspect
to me. I don't defect to happiness, but I don't demonstrate
longing in any empty square.

You collect the crumbs with a sweep of your hand,
straightening your glasses by aligning the frames with the
ears, not the lenses with the eyes, replying with the body
that you already lost, and I almost forget what I held in
my Adam's apple, clenched on the words that were once
between us. And now look at us, chatting for hours. There
is no rule about these things. I read you the winners of the
short story contest, even the jury comments. To the jury
comments you would never in your life have listened, but
I don't care, we are having a good time, the phone is on
silent, and I am not subjected to the knowledge that you
don't call. I am telling you about my life the way I tell my
friends, it's only that I happen to have more of it than you
do. The little one has learned to read; the older one still
believes that the answer will be yes. And home is the place
in which the sum total of actions outweighs the total sum
of nonactions; every morning I wake up in it, scale-crazed,
and sometimes I forget that you—and here you are shifting
your gaze.

שמרים

שׁוּבִי שׁוּבִי וְאֶחֱזֶה בַּמִּטְבָּח, אֵיךְ יָדַעְתְּ לְלַמֵּד אוֹתִי שֶׁהַקֶּמַח
הוּא הַתּוֹרָה וְהַלִּישָׁה מַרְגִּיעָה אֶת הַשְּׁמָרִים כְּמוֹ אֶת הָעֲדָרִים
לִפְנֵי הַשְּׁחִיטָה, וְשֶׁהַכְּלָלִי נִפְתָּח לַפְּרָטִי אִם אוֹמְרִים אֶת
סִיסְמַת הַיָּדַיִם, וְשֶׁבְּוָנִיל אִי אֶפְשָׁר לִרְמוֹת.

כְּשֶׁהָיִית בַּחַיִּים הָיוּ יָמִים שְׁלֵמִים שֶׁיָּכֹלְתִּי שֶׁלֹּא
לַחְשֹׁב עָלַיִךְ
וְגַם עַכְשָׁו אֲנִי יְכוֹלָה.

בְּלִי לְהוֹדוֹת בָּזֶה אֲנִי מְחַכָּה.
לֹא עוֹרֶקֶת לָאֲשֶׁר אֲבָל לֹא מַפְגִּינָה גַּעְגּוּעַ בְּשׁוּם כִּכָּר רֵיקָה,
כָּל מִי שֶׁיֵּשׁ לוֹ אִמָּא חָשׁוּד בְּעֵינַי.

אַתְּ אוֹסֶפֶת פֵּרוּרִים עִם מַגְרֶפֶת הַיָּד, מֵיטִיבָה אֶת מִשְׁקָפַיִךְ לֹא בְּמַגָּע עִם
הָעֲדָשׁוֹת אֶלָּא בְּחִבּוּר הַמִּשְׁקָף עִם הָאֹזֶן, מְשִׁיבָה לִי עִם הַגּוּף שֶׁדַּוְקָא הוּא שֶׁאָבַד
לָךְ רִאשׁוֹן. וַאֲנִי כִּמְעַט שׁוֹכַחַת מָה הֶחֱזַקְתִּי בְּאֶגְרוֹף הַגְּרוֹגֶרֶת שֶׁנִּקְפַּץ עַל הַמִּלִּים
בֵּינֵינוּ פַּעַם. זֶה לֹא שֶׁלֹּא הָיִינוּ נִפְגָּשׁוֹת אֲבָל הָעֲרֵבוּת שֶׁלָּךְ אֵלַי הָפְכָה הַכֹּל
לַחְשׁוּב, הִדְגִּישָׁה אֶת הַטָּעֻיּוֹת, וְעַכְשָׁו תִּרְאִי אוֹתָנוּ, מְפֻטְפְּטוֹת שָׁעוֹת. אֵין דִּין
בְּתוֹךְ הַדְּבָרִים. אֲנִי מַקְרִיאָה לָךְ אֶת זוֹכֵי תַּחֲרוּת הַסִּפּוּר הַקָּצָר וַאֲפִלּוּ אֶת נִמּוּקֵי
הַשּׁוֹפְטִים. לְנִמּוּקֵי הַשּׁוֹפְטִים בַּחַיִּים לֹא הָיִית מַקְשִׁיבָה אֲבָל לֹא אִכְפַּת לִי כִּי יֵשׁ
לָנוּ שָׁעָה טוֹבָה, הַטֶּלֶפוֹן עַל שָׁקֶט וַאֲנִי לֹא מְשֻׁעְבֶּדֶת לַיְדִיעָה שֶׁלֹּא תִּתְקַשְּׁרִי.
מְסַפֶּרֶת לָךְ עַל חַיַּי כְּמוֹ שֶׁאֲנִי מְסַפֶּרֶת לַחֲבֵרָה שָׁרָק בְּמִקְרֶה יֵשׁ לִי יוֹתֵר מִמֶּנָּה.
הַקְּטַנָּה לָמְדָה לִקְרֹא, הַגְּדוֹלָה עֲדַיִן יוֹתֵר מַאֲמִינָה שֶׁהַתְּשׁוּבָה תִּהְיֶה כֵּן. וְהַבַּיִת
הוּא הַמָּקוֹם שֶׁבּוֹ סַךְ הַמַּעֲשִׂים עוֹלֶה עַל סַךְ אִי-הַמַּעֲשִׂים, כָּל בֹּקֶר אֲנִי מִתְעוֹרֶרֶת
בּוֹ טְרוּפַת קַשְׁקֻשֵׁי לְסַדֵּר וְלָקַחַת לִפְעָמִים שׁוֹכַחַת שֶׁאַתְּ, מָה אֶפְשָׁר לַעֲנוֹת לָזֶה
שׁוֹכַחַת שֶׁאַתְּ, אַתְּ מְסִיטָה אֶת הַמַּבָּט.

NEW POEMS

A THOUSAND NIGHTS

And after we schlepped the blue sofa to the new flat,
and after calling all the people with Russian names we
    found in the yellow pages to ask about that game your
    grandmother used to play,
and after the winter rain fell from the ceiling but we were
    not offended with our life, we couldn't imagine what it is
    to drown,
and after the CD got stuck at the crucial moment under
    the chuppah (though I'd told you to check the sound
    system), so that suddenly, ten minutes later, Mercedes
    Sosa came on, "Gracias a la vida, gracias," and the
    guests already queued up at the buffet, plates in hand,
    refrained from throwing cooked rice at the bride,
and after the children, who appeared into the crying from
    the screaming,
and after the bills and the financial issues that accumulated
    like a disease and an ill-matching cure,
and after the YouTube slow dance party in the living room
    because we were too cheap for a babysitter on New
    Year's Eve,
and after I answered you yes, so many times and fewer
    times than I answered you no, I am boasting of that
    now like a woman who has lived her life as if it were
    literature only to discover that it was math,
and after we went to teacher-parent meetings, even though
    we didn't have to, and in the mornings we stole five
    minutes,
and after we folded all the fingers into one pointing finger,
and after we squeezed like a baby all the words to the one
    and only word, "this,"
and after I listened to the beats of your body and let the
    anxieties frighten me so that I could catch you from the
    beginning,

אֶלֶף לַיְלָה

וְאַחֲרֵי שֶׁסָּחַבְנוּ אֶת הַסַּפּוֹת הַכְּחֻלּוֹת לַדִּירָה הַחֲדָשָׁה, וְאַחֲרֵי שֶׁהִתְקַשַּׁרְנוּ
לַאֲנָשִׁים עִם שֵׁמוֹת רוּסִיִּים מִדַּפֵּי זָהָב לִשְׁאֹל עַל הַמִּשְׂחָק שֶׁסָּבְתָא שֶׁלָּךְ הָיְתָה
מְשַׂחֶקֶת, וְאַחֲרֵי הַגֶּשֶׁם שֶׁיָּרַד מֵהַתִּקְרָה בַּחֹרֶף אֲבָל לֹא נֶעֱלַבְנוּ מֵאֵיךְ שֶׁהַחַיִּים
שֶׁלָּנוּ נִרְאִים, לֹא יָכֹלְנוּ לְדַמְיֵן מָה זֶה לִטְבֹּעַ, וְאַחֲרֵי הַדִּיסְק שֶׁנִּתְקַע דַּוְקָא בַּחֻפָּה,
אָמַרְתִּי לָךְ לִבְדֹּק שֶׁהַטֵּיפּ שֶׁל הַמָּקוֹם קוֹרֵא צָרוּבִים, וְאַחֲרֵי שֶׁהַקּוֹל שֶׁל מֶרְסֶדֶס
סוֹסָה עָלָה פִּתְאֹם, לֹא קָשׁוּר: תּוֹדָה לַחַיִּים, תּוֹדָה לַחַיִּים, הָאוֹרְחִים כְּבָר עָמְדוּ
נְבוֹכִים עִם צַלָּחוֹת בַּתּוֹר לַמָּנָה, מְנוּעִים מִלִּזְרוֹת אֹרֶז מְבֻשָּׁל עַל הַכַּלָּה, וְאַחֲרֵי
הַיְלָדִים שֶׁהִגִּיחוּ אֶל הַבֶּכִי מִן הַצְּעָקָה, וְאַחֲרֵי הַחֶשְׁבּוֹנוֹת וְהַמָּמוֹנוֹת שֶׁהִצְטַבְּרוּ
כְּמַחֲלָה וּתְרוּפָה לֹא לְגַמְרֵי תּוֹאֶמֶת, וְאַחֲרֵי מְסִבַּת הַסָּלוֹאוּ מִיוּטִיוּב בַּסָּלוֹן כִּי
הִתְקַמְצַנּוּ עַל בֵּיבִּיסִיטֶר לַשָּׁנָה הַחֲדָשָׁה, וְאַחֲרֵי שֶׁהֶשַׁבְתִּי לָךְ כֵּן פְּעָמִים רַבּוֹת כָּל
כָּךְ וּפָחוֹת מִזֶּה הֶשַׁבְתִּי לָךְ לֹא, אֲנִי מִתְגָּאָה בָּזֶה עַכְשָׁו כְּמוֹ מִישֶׁהִי שֶׁחָיְתָה אֶת
חַיֶּיהָ כְּסִפְרוּת וּמְגַלָּה שֶׁהָיוּ מָתֵמָטִיקָה, וְאַחֲרֵי שֶׁהָלַכְנוּ לַאֲסֵפוֹת הוֹרִים, אֲפִלּוּ
שֶׁלֹּא חַיָּבִים, וּבַבְּקָרִים גָּנַבְנוּ חָמֵשׁ דַּקּוֹת שֶׁבָּהֶן הָעֵינַיִם הַיְרֻקּוֹת שֶׁלָּךְ הָפְנוּ אֵלַי
לְדַקָּה, וְאַחֲרֵי שֶׁקִּפַּלְנוּ אֶת כָּל הָאֶצְבָּעוֹת לְאֶצְבַּע אַחַת מַצְבִּיעָה, וְאַחֲרֵי שֶׁדָּחַסְנוּ
כְּמוֹ תִּינוֹק אֶת כָּל הַמִּלִּים לַמִּלָּה הַיְחִידָה 'זֶה', וְאַחֲרֵי שֶׁהִקְשַׁבְתִּי לִפְעִימוֹת
גּוּפֵךְ, וְנָתַתִּי לַחֲרָדוֹת לְהַבְהִיל אוֹתִי אוֹתִי כְּדֵי שֶׁאוּכַל לִתְפֹּס אוֹתֵךְ מֵהַתְחָלָה, וְלוּ רַק

if only it were possible to stop with this, to hold on to the thousand as if they were ten thousand, but just tonight and a night that tells us as a tale, seducing us here, tomorrow, too, unafraid to continue, until in the end the great fatigue is what will kill us like a king, and after all this, we didn't notice that it arrived, but it is already at the soft pillow, waiting to strangle from behind, and its hand is sliding, slowly, to the nape of the neck.

אֶפְשָׁר הָיָה לַעֲצֹר בָּזֶה, לְהַחְזִיק אֶת הָאֶלֶף כְּאִלּוּ הוּא רְבָבָה, אֲבָל דַּוְקָא הַלַּיְלָה
וְלַיְלָה שֶׁמְּסַפֵּר אוֹתָנוּ כְּמַעֲשִׂיָּה, מְפַתֶּה אוֹתָנוּ לִהְיוֹת פֹּה גַּם מָחָר, בְּלִי לְפַחֵד מִן
הַהֶמְשֵׁךְ, עַד שֶׁבַּסּוֹף הָעֲיֵפוּת הַגְּדוֹלָה הִיא שֶׁתַּהֲרֹג אוֹתָנוּ כְּמֶלֶךְ, גַּם אִם שְׁנֵינוּ
נִחְיֶה. לֹא שַׂמְנוּ לֵב שֶׁהִגִּיעָה, אֲבָל הִיא כְּבָר בַּכָּרִית הָרַכָּה. מְחַכָּה לַחְנֹק מֵהַצַּד
שֶׁל הָעֹרֶף, אַחֲרֵי כָּל זֶה, לְאַט וּמִצְטַבֵּר.

CHILD

You come out into the living room past your bedtime
bearing the passport of the simple question
that always begins, what does it mean, and always turns
into, that's not how to answer.

I have almost nothing with which to answer you, my child,
I don't know what orders the periodic table,
nor what lies beyond outer space, if anything does,
but facing you I feel
that there isn't really much more for me to learn,
that maybe I've even arrived.

And when you drag your dwarfish feet
back to bed, they seem giant.
I know that now in the years to come I can be still,
not needing to say please,
only standing outside your door
while you read and fall asleep.

Something does lie beyond outer space, child, just so
    you know,
and for its sake I am reaching for the light above your head,
turning it on, then off, and then on again,
winking at the stars from inside the house.

ילד

אַתָּה יוֹצֵא לַסָּלוֹן אַחֲרֵי שְׁעַת הַהַשְׁכָּבָה,
נוֹשֵׂא כְּדַרְכְּךָ אֶת הַשְּׁאֵלָה הַפְּשׁוּטָה
שֶׁמַּתְחִילָה תָּמִיד בְּמָה זֹאת אוֹמֶרֶת וּמִסְתַּיֶּמֶת
בְּכָכָה זֶה לֹא תְּשׁוּבָה.

אֲנִי לֹא יוֹדַעַת לַעֲנוֹת לְךָ כִּמְעַט עַל כְּלוּם, יֶלֶד,
לֹא מָה מְסַדֵּר אֶת הַטַּבְלָה הַמַּחְזוֹרִית
וְלֹא מָה מֵאֲחוֹרֵי הֶחָלָל וְאִם יֵשׁ בִּכְלָל,
אֲבָל מוּלְךָ אֲנִי מַרְגִּישָׁה
שֶׁכְּבָר אֵין לִי עוֹד כָּל כָּךְ הַרְבֵּה לִלְמֹד
וַאֲפִלּוּ יִתָּכֵן שֶׁהִגַּעְתִּי.

וּכְשֶׁאַתָּה גּוֹרֵר אֶת רַגְלֶיךָ חֲזָרָה לַמִּטָּה,
גַּמָּד לְמַבָּט, עֲנָק לָזוֹ שֶׁמַּבִּיטָה,
אֲנִי יוֹדַעַת שֶׁשָּׁנִים אֲנִי יְכוֹלָה לִשְׁתֹּק עַכְשָׁו
בְּלִי לְהַגִּיד בְּבַקָּשָׁה,
שָׁנִים אֲנִי יְכוֹלָה רַק לְהַקְשִׁיב לְךָ מֵעֵבֶר לַדֶּלֶת,
קוֹרֵא וְאָז נִרְדָּם.

יֵשׁ מַשֶּׁהוּ אַחֲרֵי הֶחָלָל, יֶלֶד, רַק שֶׁתֵּדַע,
וַאֲנִי נִגֶּשֶׁת בִּשְׁבִילוֹ לָאוֹר שֶׁמֵּעַל רֹאשֵׁךְ,
מְכַבָּה, מַדְלִיקָה, וְשׁוּב מְכַבָּה,
קוֹרֶצֶת לַכּוֹכָבִים מִתּוֹךְ הַבַּיִת.

NOTES ON THE POEMS

My Beloved

Gidali's poem in Hebrew employs parallelism, such as is found in much Biblical poetry. The inverted sentence structure in the opening lines (exaggerated in the original Hebrew) draws attention to the parallel symbols and rhythms of each line. This particular poem echoes, in its themes and narrative, Song of Songs 1:13–14; its praises of the beloved in terms of pastoral imagery is similar to Song of Songs 2; and Song of Songs 5 is echoed in the lover's anticipation of the beloved at the door. Gidali's poem draws attention to the absence of the Song of Songs' "daughters of Jerusalem," as the speaker can only dream of having a retinue, i.e., money to hire girls to envy her.

The last stanza of the first section (to lay my ribs / in the space between his ribs / and I return to him) refers to the fact that Eve was created from Adam's rib in the second creation narrative, Genesis 2:21–23.

An etrog is the fragrant yellow citron that is used ritually by Jews during the week of Sukkot. Because the fruit must be without blemish, during the holiday it is often stored in a special box and protected with padding.

The "seven bad years" refers to Genesis 41:29–30, in which Joseph, while incarcerated in Egypt, interprets the Pharaoh's dream, accurately depicting a famine.

Note

The laws of kashrut, Jewish dietary restrictions, prohibit the mixing of milk and meat, in accordance with the command not to boil a calf in its mother's milk.

Hard Morning

In Hungarian, *puszi* means "kiss," which, in Hebrew, sounds like the American slang "pussy."

Psalm

The poem echoes the Book of Psalms in structure and vocabulary. Many of the psalms are prefaced in Hebrew with the phrase "A psalm in honor of David" and have instructions for their purpose and the musical accompaniment. Gidali replaces God or David with human activity as the object of praise. The second part of this poem seems to echo the songs of personal lament, in which enemies and dangers are enumerated, such as in Psalm 59:1–17, whose speaker is David asking protection from Saul, who is attempting to kill him. As in Biblical poetry, Gidali structures this poem using parallelism: "A psalm of waking up for money, a psalm of victors," etc.

That Girl

The last line is a corruption of Psalm 72:19, "the whole earth is filled with the glory of God."

Sarah Laughed Again

This poem is spoken from the perspective of Isaac, whom Abraham took to Mount Moriah to be sacrificed to God. God stays Abraham's hand at the last moment (Genesis 22:6–13). Sarah dies, presumably from grief, before Abraham returns with the living Isaac. The poem also refers to the fact that when Sarah was told she would bear a child in her advanced age, she laughed (Genesis 18:12–15). Isaac's name, in Hebrew, means "he will laugh" (Genesis 21:3–6).

Kohelet

Kohelet is the Hebrew name of Ecclesiastes, and refers to the author as well as the book. Tradition assigns the identity of Kohelet to Solomon, son of David. Solomon famously had 700 royal wives and 300 concubines (1 Kings 11:3).

Isaac

The Torah portion that relates the life of Abraham before the birth of Isaac is called Lech Lecha, for the opening words, which mean "Go!" (Genesis 12:1–17:27). It ends with God creating a covenant with Abraham through circumcision and is the beginning of God's relationship with the Jewish people. In the Bible in general, and in this portion in particular, words and phrases are doubled in Hebrew for emphasis, or to create commands.

Samson and Absalom

Both of these Biblical figures received their strength and their downfall through their hair. Samson (Judges 13–16) was dedicated by his parents to God before his conception as a Nazirite, meaning he was to abstain from alcoholic drink and he must never cut his hair. According to the Book of Judges, God gave Samson extrahuman strength to fight the Philistines. Delilah, the second beloved woman who betrayed him to the Philistines, had Samson's hair shaved off while he slept on her lap, and he was captured and blinded. After his hair grew back, he prayed for his strength to return and then pushed apart the marble pillars of the temple in Gaza where the Philistines had gathered to thank their god Dagon for delivering Samson into their hands.

Absalom was the third son of King David (his full sister, Tamar, is discussed in the poem "We Could Have Lived So Well, You Say, and Gaze at Her, Still Pretty"). He was called the most beautiful man in the kingdom; his charm and good looks seemed to have tempted him to rebel against his father. In battle his hair got caught in an oak tree and he was lifted from his horse. His father's men found him dangling from the tree by his hair and a rival ordered him killed, against his father's wishes. His story appears in 2 Samuel 3:3, and 2 Samuel 2:13–18.

Songs to a Dead Woman

Your Daughter (2.)

For the line "Behold, who is this that cometh up from the kindergarten," see Song of Songs 2:8, "Behold he cometh leaping upon the mountains, skipping upon the hills."

Your Daughter (3.)

"Two consonants of a word / written with diacritical marks": Hebrew words are composed of a three-letter consonant base. Vowels are indicated by diacritical marks, which are patterns of dots usually placed above or below the consonants. Diacritical marks are generally used only for poetry and children's books.

Your Husband (4.)

"Rachel and Leah" refers to Genesis 29:16–30, in which Jacob works seven years in order to marry Rachel, whom he loves, but then he is deceived into marrying Rachel's older sister, Leah. He is then given Rachel, after seven more years of labor. This begins a rivalry that ends only after the two sisters have conceived the twelve sons that will represent the twelve tribes of Israel. See Genesis 29:31–30:25.

God of Straw Mothers

This English translation is lineated in the tradition of English translations of Biblical poetry, especially the psalms, to enhance the effect of parallelism, and to mark it as poetry. These psalms in Hebrew are traditionally presented in block text, as in Gidali's original. For more on literary translation of Biblical poetry, see Yosefa Raz's chapter "Seraphic Song and the Stutters of the Visionary Poet: Robert Lowth's Eighteenth-Century Re-invention of Prophecy" in her forthcoming *Prophecy, Power, and Weakness: A Cultural History of the Bible in Modernity* (Indiana University Press).

"Hatikva" [The Hope] is the national anthem of Israel. It is adapted from Naftali Herz Imber's nine-stanza, 1878 romantic poem "Tikvatenu" [Our Hope], which he wrote after the establishment of Petah Tikva, one of the first Jewish settlements in Ottoman Palestine. The lyrics were modified several times; its current melody was composed by Samuel Cohen in 1888. Cohen seems to have adapted his melody from one of the Eastern European variants of Gasparo Zanetti's "La

Mantovana," such as the Czech Bendrich Smetana's "Vlatava," from his composition *Ma Vlast* [My Homeland], or the contemporaneous Romanian, Ukrainian, or Polish folk songs that used that tune. Notable moments in the song's history include 1919, when it was banned in British Mandate Palestine, and 1948, when it was adopted unofficially as the national anthem of the State of Israel. There were often other contenders for the national anthem, some of which sought to correct the song's description of "the longing of the Jewish soul" for Zion, in recognition that not all the souls in the State of Israel are Jewish. "Hatikva" was made official only in 2004.

We Could Have Lived So Well, You Say, and Gaze at Her, Still Pretty

During Shabbat, which is from sunset on Friday night until an hour after sunset on Saturday night, all work ceases for religiously observant Jews. Friday and Saturday officially comprise an Israeli weekend.

The Plain of Sharon stretches from the Yarkon River, at the northern boundary of Tel Aviv, to Haifa and Mt. Carmel in the north, and from the Mediterranean Sea to the hills of Samaria. This coastal plain is the most densely populated area of Israel. Biblical references appear in 1 Chronicles 5:16, 27:29; Isaiah 33:9, 35:2, 65:10; and Song of Songs 2:1.

Tamar is the daughter of King David and the full sister of Absalom; she was raped by her lustful half-brother Amnon, who immediately developed an intense hatred for her and refused her legal or material compensation (2 Samuel 13). In Hebrew, the pansy flower is called "Amnon and Tamar."

Etrog

Shmita is the sabbatical year in the seven-year agricultural cycle, during which time the land is left fallow. All agricultural activity, including plowing, planting, pruning, and harvesting, is forbidden by Jewish law.

For the significance of the etrog, see the note on "My Beloved," above.

Heir to the Curfew

Mount Moriah is where, according to Jewish tradition, the binding of Isaac occurs. According to Islam, the son is Ishmael, not Isaac. In both cases, the angel of God stays Abraham's hand, and a ram is sacrificed instead of the son.

"Waters of Meribah" appears in Exodus 17:1–7. Here the Israelites, newly liberated from Egyptian slavery and wandering in the desert, are grumbling against God because they have no water. God tells Moses to take elders with him and smite the rock so that water will flow, and Moses calls the place Meribah, which, he says, means "quarreling" or "testing." In Numbers 20:1–24 the story is repeated, but here God tells Moses and Aaron to speak to the rock. Because Moses strikes it, instead, to make the waters flow, God tells Moses he is not permitted to enter the land that God promised to his people.

The woman from the lock company calls to ask

The phrase "the taxes of my hands have been thrown into the sea" is, according to Rabbi Jonathan, the Babylonian Talmud, Tractate Sanhedrin, folio 39b, a play on God's words of rebuke to the angels, who asked God's permission to sing a song of praise as the Egyptians were being drowned in the Sea of Reeds in pursuit of the Israelites (Exodus 14). God tells the angels, "The work of my hands is drowned in the sea," questioning why, then, they would sing praise, and implying that the occasion, rather, calls for sorrow. God's words also mirror Moses and Miriam's song of praise (Exodus 15:1–21).

The line *if a man comes to kill you, rise early* . . . is taken from the Babylonian Talmud, Tractate Berakoth, folio 58a. The end of the quote is "and kill him first."

Ne'ila is the concluding prayer of the Yom Kippur (Day of Atonement) service. It is the last chance to seal God's judgment for a good year, or to overturn a bad judgment. The closing of the doors of the ark of the covenant symbolizes the closing of heaven's gates to prayer and petitions, for the purposes of overturning a bad judgment for the year.

I am Isaac in reverse

By the end of Isaac's life he had gone blind; thus he was tricked into blessing Jacob instead of Esau, the firstborn. The poem also references the apple of the Garden of Eden and the "formlessness and void" of Genesis 1:2.

Toward morning I found a blind cat

The words *soldiers   soldiers   fire   our village devoured* refer to the Russian pogroms and Kristallnacht. The word "devour," used in Holocaust literature, specifically echoes Genesis 37:20 and 37:33, in which Joseph's brothers plot to kill Joseph, saying that a wild animal devoured him. Gidali's poem portrays the people who had once been devoured like Joseph as the potential devourers of those who live in refugee camps.

Boy, there is peat from under the swamp

Though Esau was Isaac's favorite, and the first born of the twin sons, their mother, Rebecca, helped Jacob steal Esau's blessing by covering Jacob's forearms with goatskins and instructing Jacob to feed Isaac the meal Isaac asked Esau to prepare for him; thereby tricking the blind Isaac into blessing Jacob instead of Esau.

Jacob, in turn, was tricked by Laban into marrying Leah, when he thought he was marrying Rachel, whom he loved. He had to labor fourteen years for his father-in-law, seven for each of the sisters he married. Joseph, Rachel's son, was betrayed by his brothers and sold into slavery. It was this treachery against Joseph that saved the Israelites during a time of famine. It was also the treachery that made them become slaves in the land of Egypt. For the story of Esau and Jacob, see Genesis 27:1–40; for Jacob, Leah, and Rachel, see Genesis 29:1–30; for Joseph and his brothers, Genesis 37:1–35.

The Love, Yonatan

The Rilke translation from German into English is mine.

For the relationship between Yonatan, son of King Saul, and David, slayer of Goliath, see 1 Samuel 18:1–4 and 2 Samuel 1:23–27. Yonatan and David ought to have been rivals; in fact, Saul feared David's popularity and sought to kill him. David succeeded Saul as king upon Yonatan's death in battle and Saul's subsequent suicide.

3.

"Yonatan, Yehonatan, Yonatan, / where God comes out of his name": The name Yonatan means "God has given." The letters that are removed from the name Yehonatan to create the contracted form, Yonatan, are the letters used to indicate one of God's names. Both names refer to Yonatan, son of Saul and friend of David.

4.

"Ten percent offering" refers to the obligatory tithe from Biblical times; it is practiced today among religious Jews in the form of giving ten percent of one's monetary income to charity.

5.

King David's betrayal of Uriah the Hittite, one of his thirty-seven best fighters, is documented in 2 Samuel 11. David saw Uriah's wife, Bathsheba, bathing in her courtyard and had her brought to him. After she became pregnant, he summoned Uriah from battle so that he might stay the night with her. When Uriah's code of honor compelled him to refuse David's request, David arranged for Uriah to fall in battle. This was a crime that displeased God (2 Samuel 12), and Absalom's rebellion is seen as a punishment. David and Bathsheba's second child was King Solomon.

6.

In 1 Samuel 18:24–25 Saul asks David for the foreskins of 100 slain Philistines as a bride price for his daughter Micha. Saul hoped that David would be killed in the undertaking, but David brought back 200 foreskins instead.

9.

Saul, the name of the king, is pronounced Shaul in Hebrew, and in Hebrew the name means "borrowed."

Reverse Sati

Sati refers to the (now illegal) Hindi funeral ritual whereby a widowed woman would immolate herself on her husband's funeral pyre. The Hindi and Sanskrit term referred to a "chaste woman," or "good wife."

The line "but he who takes a fire to his bosom will not be impoverished" is from Proverbs 6:27.

The quote "All the world is a very narrow bridge and the main thing is not to be afraid" is attributed to Rabbi Nachman of Breslav. Set to music, it has been sung by most of the legendary Israeli musicians.